Breaking the barriers to business growth

A compilation of expert insights into growing your business

Edited by Sarah Williams
Paul Ovington & Albert Wright

Breaking the barriers to business growth
Copyright ©2012 Right Angle Consultants
Published in 2012 by Busi Books

The views expressed in each chapter are solely those of the individual author and do
not necessarily represent a collective view.

A CIP record for this book is available from the British Library.

ISBN 978-0-9571461-0-5

Designed and produced by Sue Richardson Associates   www.suerichardson.co.uk

Printed and bound in Great Britain by TJ International, Padstow, Cornwall.

Contents

Testimonials

"Grounded in solid theoretical business concepts, *Breaking the Barriers to Business Growth* provides entrepreneurs with strategic frameworks that not only help to clarify the root of challenges existing in the current economic climate, but to formulate strategies to overcome challenges and achieve business success. As an entrepreneur I found this book useful in holistically examining and addressing relevant issues and providing tangible methods for improving the bottom line."

Julianne Kissack RN, MBA (Saïd Business School), Healthcare Consultant, Professional Motivational Speaker/Coach, Founder of Speaking for Success Vancouver, Canada

"We tend to read the books that fit our view of the world (like the papers we choose to read). *Breaking the Barriers to Business Growth*, on the other hand, has stuff we want to find out about but also the things we don't want to find out about and I see that as a huge plus. Because this book has everything in one place, little tasters and teases on all the key topics, most people will read their fave subjects and skim 'the rest'. However you get an irking feeling that you should be reading 'the rest'. This book, somehow, gets you to look at 'the rest', all those topics you know you should be up to speed on but have somehow managed to avoid confronting. Hats off to the BB2BG team."

Robert Craven, Author & Keynote Speaker

"This book helps to open up opportunities and give you the answers to your business challenges. It can be used at any stage you are, at new start up or having been in business for a time."

Harry Fletcher, Partner in the first ecco shoe franchise in UK and director of ecco oxford Ltd

"This book is a great starting point for small businesses, as it provides an overview on various areas and opportunities of growth. Business owners will gain ideas for igniting growth in their respective businesses, as well as invaluable access to personal services by the authors."

Jennifer Tan, MBA, University of Oxford, Specialisms: consulting, marketing, strategic planning, management

"If you are starting up a business this is an excellent, easy to read book, packed with practical advice, which will also spark new thinking and guide you to additional resources to help you."

Graham Oddey OBE, Advisor and Managing Director of Swinbrook Consulting Ltd

"It's not difficult to start a small business. What is difficult is taking that business to the point where it is self-sustaining and and providing you with a decent income without you having to kill yourself working. Take a moment to step off the treadmill and use this book to work out what you need to do for sustained success."

Alastair Dryburgh, Consultant, speaker and author, CEO, Akenhurst Consultants

"An immensely informative book with advice that if applied will change the performance of any business. Highly recommended."

Richard Denny, Author of Selling to Win *and Business Growth Specialist*

"I liked the idea of creating a general reference book covering a range of typical business issues. Particular chapters that caught my interest were Chapter 8 on SEO – I thought this chapter was really clear, honest and thorough, with some useful guidelines which I will certainly apply myself – and, amongst many others, the chapter on 'Making Sales without Selling'. It's a chapter I'll be giving to all my account managers!"

Joe Kennard, BA Hons, PGCF, Owner & MD Purple Media Ltd

RIGHT ANGLE
CONSULTANTS

Want to get a handle on getting ahead?

Running a business, especially a rapidly growing business, can be like juggling with jelly while making your way across a racing stream just on the brink of a waterfall… bewildering, exhausting and requiring your unremitting attention if things aren't going to collapse in a nasty, mucky mess.

The basic issue is that running an expanding business needs you to be an expert in so many different areas – human resource management, finance, marketing, strategy, IT and, now, even social media. How can any one person be expert in all of these key areas? Well, the truth is, it's almost impossible.

No doubt, as a business owner, you already possess an impressive array of skills and know-how. But the spectrum of skills required to be successful is very broad, and seems to be getting broader every day. As business owners we can't afford to hang about – we need to get along the learning curve quickly, without squandering time, money and energy trying to pick up everything through our own hard experience.

Here at Right Angle Consultants we have devised a convenient solution to many entrepreneurial challenges. We offer educational support and help in all the important aspects of business management and growth. We have assembled some formidable expertise that you can conveniently tap into. As illustrated in this book, we can offer help in many different aspects of running a business.

Check out our website at www.right-angle-consultants.co.uk to get the latest information on training, books, blogs, consultancy and courses – and much more besides.

Special offer: For readers of Breaking the Barriers to Business Growth, each month we make a special educational offer to help you in your quest to expand and run a successful business. Claim your gift by visiting: www.right-angle-consultants.co.uk/helpmybusiness

Let us help you get the Right Angle on your business.

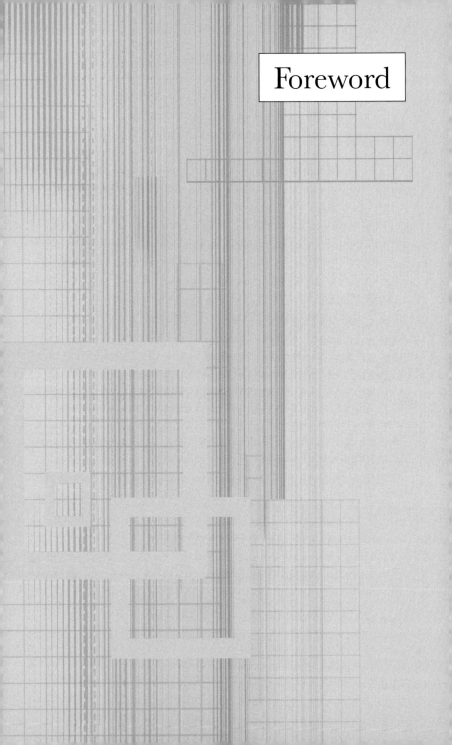

Foreword

Foreword

Janette Faherty, OBE, BA, MPhil, FRSA, FCMI. Director Avanta Enterprise Limited

Many business books fall down because the author tries to cover too much ground and present expertise in areas where, quite frankly, they are not experts. *Breaking the Barriers to Business Growth* contains 13 chapters of relevant, practical advice by experts within their field. Having chaired a workshop, where a number of the book's authors presented in 2011, I was impressed not only by their knowledge but by their enthusiasm and passion for supporting people growing their businesses.

Having grown a successful business myself I can attest that there are some excellent and thought provoking ideas and suggestions contained in *Breaking the Barriers*, and some questions which, looking back, make me embarrassed that I might not have been able to answer as well as I should or perhaps did not realise the importance of at an early enough stage. The chapters on improving cash flow for example, how to cost and price and the chapter on the importance of using management accounts to identify how well parts of the business are really doing, are so crucial. In the modern business world it is also important to understand the use of social media and how to drive customers to your website. Having worked with a number of smaller businesses, I have often had to explain how crucial it is to build a brand which reflects not only your product/service but truly and authentically reflects your values.

If you are reading *Breaking the Barriers* as an aid to growing your business, we wish you every success. Use the information and practical advice in this book and most importantly take ACTION as appropriate for your business.

This book is a unique and valuable resource on its own and having read the chapters, I encourage you to go on and read the individual books written by the authors, attend their training seminars or consult them as advisers.

Introduction

Introduction

A little while ago a light bulb switched on in my head. The idea was to create a multi-author book, each author being a recognised expert in their respective business field and with all chapters aligned along a single theme – how to break the barriers to business growth. I discussed the concept with my Right Angle business partners, Sarah Williams and Albert Wright. As a group, we didn't hesitate to accept the concept and swiftly turned it into a live project. This book is the result.

It is a well known fact that the economy is progressively seeing a greater number of small businesses and new start-ups. The ones that make it through the infantile mortality stage often have potential to grow further. It is the hope and intention of central and local governments and local communities that businesses will grow, take on new employees and boost the economy. However, few business owners have been through the growth cycle before and, more than likely, they will not be equipped to create and manage rapid growth. There is therefore a natural barrier that small companies have to break through in order to get their business to the next level.

As a business owner or business leader you will no doubt have a great deal of know-how and a key set of skills. Growing a business rapidly, however, requires a very wide spectrum of skills and every business owner inevitably has some skill gaps.

Each of the chapter authors in this book is an expert in at least one field. They have been hand-picked for their experience and the deep insights they have gained by specialising in specific areas. In this book, *Breaking the Barriers to Business Growth*, you have at your fingertips their knowledge and wisdom, which have invariably taken the experts years to accumulate. We can't all hope to gain such wisdom independently, so why not share it? By tapping into these insights you can take years off your learning experience.

We encourage you to read all the chapters and use the know-how in your own business. If you need more information or help then each of the authors has given a specific offer of assistance. We also encourage you to get involved in the Right Angle community by visiting our website at www.right-angle-consultants.co.uk.

Paul Ovington MBA, MSc, DipM

Chapter 1

Creating business success through strategy

Paul Ovington

Creating business success through strategy
Paul Ovington

Welcome to the new white-water world!

You may have noticed how turbulent and dynamic the world has become. This is particularly true of the business environment and the way businesses work. Arguably, the root cause of this turbulence is advancement in silicon technology. This increases speed, reduces power, while increasing complexity per chip. The increasing functionality of silicon devices has given rise to a rapidly advancing computer and communication infrastructure.

Turbulence is now the new business norm

Information is now being processed in radically more sophisticated ways and everyone and everything is becoming connected. The global communication infrastructure is spreading. Computational power is increasing, particularly in portable devices. These developments are changing the way we work, collaborate and compete. Search engine technology and social media sophistication are also transforming how the whole marketing and sales processes function.

Besides technological changes, we have the emergence of new economic super powers such as India and China. We have financial turmoil, particularly the credit crisis, sovereign debt and shaky currencies, all leading to severe austerity measures. We also have new generations of buyers and decision makers whose buying attitudes, values and behaviour are different from those of previous generations.

The net effect of these factors is that we are facing economic upheaval, shifts in global power and new methods of competing and working. We have alarmingly rapid obsolescence, and competition is coming from all directions! What does this mean for the modern-day entrepreneur? Fundamentally, it means that we have to think strategically and move faster. We need to be constantly aware of competition, and we need to predict market changes.

The modern-day entrepreneur therefore needs to be a proficient business strategist. He needs to lead and inspire change and encourage a market-centred, value-based mindset. This places substantial new demands on all business owners.

What kind of entrepreneur are you?

The net effect of upheaval and change is that market lifecycles are considerably shorter than previously experienced. The table below summarises changes in the business environment:

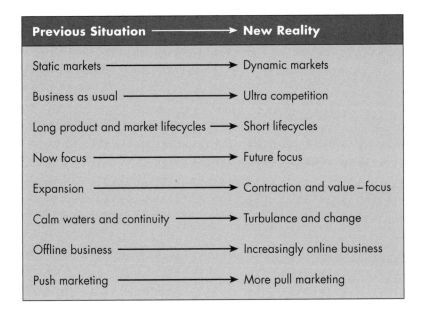

Previous Situation	New Reality
Static markets	Dynamic markets
Business as usual	Ultra competition
Long product and market lifecycles	Short lifecycles
Now focus	Future focus
Expansion	Contraction and value – focus
Calm waters and continuity	Turbulance and change
Offline business	Increasingly online business
Push marketing	More pull marketing

Given that the business environment is progressively becoming more dynamic in nature, it's worth reviewing which type of entrepreneurs can exist in various scenarios.

	Static Entrepreneur	**Dynamic Entrepreneur**
Static Environment	Optimist	Opportunist
Dynamic Environment	Risk Taker	Survivor & Thriver

Static Entrepreneur *(tends to do the same as always)*

> Static Environment: The 'Optimist', who hopes that nothing will change

> Dynamic Environment: The 'Risk Taker', who prays for survival

Dynamic Entrepreneur *(looks for opportunity to change and to seize advantage)*

> Static Environment: The 'Opportunist', who runs circles around the competition

> Dynamic Environment: The 'Survivor and Thriver', who manages to keep pace or to move ahead

The appropriate style for the modern-day entrepreneur is 'dynamic'. In this case, you are ready to change and indeed anticipate and monitor change in the business environment. As a dynamic entrepreneur you will be critically aware of both business opportunities and risks.

Winning in business

The successful entrepreneur is always winning in business, but what does 'winning' actually mean? The following six criteria for this term are worth considering:

- Business is constantly profitable

- The profit is rewarding for the effort

- There is an adequate cash balance and positive cashflow

- A stronger competitive positioning is attained

- Operates in sufficient growth markets or niches

- Has increasing asset value

If a business owner can achieve and maintain all of these outcomes, then he is truly 'winning'. If one of the six criteria is not met, then the situation is cause for concern. Naturally, in a dynamic business environment being strategically alert and agile are the critical skills required to maintain all of these conditions.

The vital concept of value

Understanding the concept of value and value creation is absolutely fundamental to building and maintaining business success. The total company value or 'value add' is the sum of all the sales minus all the costs. The costs include overhead or fixed cost, plus the variable costs associated with the products or services sold. If we achieve a positive 'value add' then we are essentially adding value to the economy as a whole. The value added is more or less the same as profitability. The value added is determined by three things:

- The pricing at which the company is able to sell products or services

- Sales volume

- The total costs of producing those products and services, including overhead costs

The value of any particular product or service is to a large extent determined by the value that the customer perceives, that is, the price he is willing to pay. It is worth noting that effective branding is an important aspect of customer value perception.

When a prospective customer decides to purchase a product or service, several mental evaluations or purchasing considerations will take place. Some of these considerations will be conscious and some may be sub-conscious in the customer's mind. These considerations will include:

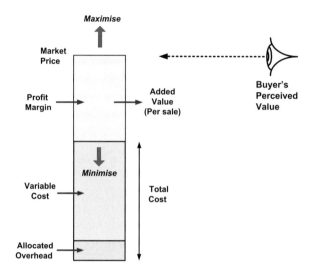

Value generation and customer value perception

- Is the asking price a reasonable price for the supplier to charge?

- Does making the purchase at this price add value to my business, that is, does it increase my overall profitability and by how much?

- Is a similar product or service available from somewhere else at a lower price?

- How unique is this product or service?

- What are the risks of going with this supplier?

- Does this purchase satisfy some of my psychological needs? (often sub-conscious)

As a business owner, seeing the offer from the prospective customer's perspective can give you a distinct advantage and should determine which products and services you develop. Your development decisions will also cover what product attributes you include, how you differentiate from other suppliers and which target markets you select. We have to almost literally 'get in the customer's shoes' in order to determine these.

If we take consideration #2 above, then gaining understanding as to how to make your customer more profitable is a distinct advantage. In another situation where we decide to develop similar products to other suppliers, based on consideration #3, we can anticipate that prices will be eroded and profit margins will be slim. It is therefore desirable to accentuate differentiation in the product or service design. If we think about the customer's consideration #4, we would probably develop product or service demonstrations, give customer testimonials or offer guarantees. All of these would reduce the customer's perception of risk.

There are several ways of enhancing the perceived value and **maximising** price:

- Augment a product or service with other valuable services, such as training – note that the effective cost to you could be far less than the added value perceived by the customer

- Add or accentuate differentiating factors in key areas

- Select target markets which really appreciate your value

- Design the product or service to improve the customer's profitability significantly

- Prove or demonstrate the value of the product or service and remove risk

- Offer some psychological benefit such as total convenience, increasing self-esteem or removing worry

The second way of improving our own 'value add' is actually to **minimise** our own costs. This could be done in a number of ways:

- Streamlining the development or production process

- Reducing wastage through quality drives

- Increasing volume

- Outsourcing some aspect of development or delivery

- Using joint venture to reduce marketing costs, that is, either cross-marketing or indirect selling with sales commission

- Removing some expensive aspects of the product or service, which are non-essential

As a business owner, developing a strong appreciation of value is fundamental to building a profitable and competitive business. A strategic plan to improve the business might therefore involve one of the following:

- Optimising the value activities to enhance the perceived value delivered

- Streamlining company overhead activities to reduce cost or to enhance delivery capability

- Optimising the target market's profitability, thereby improving your attractiveness

- Choosing a more appropriate or more attractive market

- Adding product or service differentiation

- Bundling or un-bundling products or services to offer a desirable solution that some market segment would appreciate

- Developing joint ventures to either improve what is delivered or to extend the target market

Evidently, there are many options to improve a company's delivered value. There are indeed plenty of advantages from becoming a dynamic entrepreneur and building superior value.

The strategic triangle

We have talked about the customer and our own company, but what about the competition? In his book, *Mind of the Strategist*, Kenicho Ohmae introduced the powerful concept of the three 'C's. These were:

- Company

- Customer

- Competition

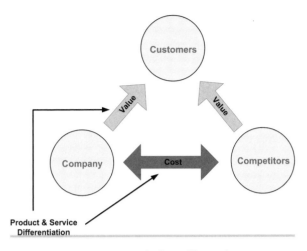

The Strategic Triangle devised by K.Ohmae

What Dr Ohmae emphasised was that when deriving a future development strategy, we must consider all three entities in order to be successful. First and foremost we must consider the customer or, more exactly, a particular group of customers, often referred to as a market segment. However, we also have to consider our own strengths and weaknesses. It is smarter to pursue a strategy based on our natural strengths rather than on our weaknesses. Thirdly, we have to consider the competition. Which competitors already serve our desired target market? If we are weaker than them, can we define a niche where we can identify customer needs that we can satisfy, but the competition can't or perhaps there exists a niche they don't particularly care about? If we are initially similar to the competition then we need to somehow differentiate.

If the competitors are offering similar services or products then the customer's buying decision is likely to be determined by price, reducing profit. This is where achieving smarter differentiation needs to be a key part of our development strategy. This goes hand-in-hand with intelligent market targeting.

Whatever strategic moves we undertake then some in-depth analysis of the three entities is required first. Neither customers nor competition are static and market situations can change quite rapidly. This dynamic nature of markets and competition means that we as entrepreneurs need to be more strategically aware and dynamic. We also need to be more aggressive with our company development plans, otherwise we might be outdone by a more agile competitor.

A modern-day skills framework for dynamic entrepreneurs

Effective entrepreneurs need to choose a direction which improves competitive standing, while satisfying customer needs and differentiating in profitable ways. The demands on business owners are far greater than they used to be. To help you with meeting these new challenges I have defined a new framework, which will enable you to survive and thrive in a turbulent and ultra-competitive environment.

The framework consists of eight critical skill areas. In each skill area you need to achieve a degree of competence, if not mastery. The more skill areas you can master, the more successful you will be in business. It is as simple as that. The figure below illustrates the framework:

The new framework for strategic skills

Let us just run through each of the eight skills in this new framework, which I have entitled, the 'Entrepreneur's New Strategic Mission'.

Skill 1: Asset accumulation

Assets in the past were conventionally defined as land, premises and equipment. An expanded view of assets includes know-how, website, customer base, products, services, technologies and considerably more. Assets are things which allow us to maintain and grow a profitable business. They also allow us to be competitive. Developing assets on a continuous basis is a very smart thing to do.

Skill 2: Value creation

Identifying areas where we can create value for customers by satisfying their needs, by reducing their costs or by increasing the value customers themselves can deliver. We can create value by numerous means, including differentiating and joint venturing.

Skill 3: Innovation

We can also innovate in numerous ways including by defining new target markets, product design, service design and creating novel business model definitions.

Skill 4: Development

Development is a deliberate change process, which helps build our competitiveness. This includes product development, market development, process or system development and relationship development. We should also include development of the company's capabilities.

Skill 5: Competitive positioning

Defining where we sit in the competitive landscape. This has a significant bearing on how profitable we become.

Skill 6: Differentiation

Understanding customer needs very precisely and identifying ways in which we can differ from our competitors. This will determine how much business we will win and what margins we can achieve.

Skill 7: Marketing

Marketing has always been a huge area, but in recent years the field has just got bigger as online marketing and social media have become prevalent factors. Choosing an optimal promotional mix from a very large array of possibilities is crucial.

Skill 8: Leverage creation

There are scores of ways we can use leverage. This means creating more business from what we already have. We can leverage off our customer base by introducing new products. We can form joint ventures and leverage off our partners' strengths. We can leverage off existing technologies and product design to create new related products.

Conclusion

We have highlighted that the world has changed and markets are far more turbulent with shorter lifecycles. Competition is coming from every angle. Being static is no longer an option. As entrepreneurs we have to become more effective strategists and more dynamic in our thinking and actions. We have introduced a framework for essential strategic skills. This is just a surface level introduction and deeper insights to some vital skill areas can be gained by referring to my Profile & Offer page (p 25).

Paul Ovington MBA, DipM, MSc, PRINCE2, MSP, DTM
Expertise Focus: Strategy & Project Management

Paul is Director of Oxford Management Solutions Ltd; a company dedicated to helping organisations of all sizes achieve strategic objectives. He is a true expert in the fields of business strategy, project management and high-tech engineering. He holds an MSc in Silicon Chip Design, an MBA and a Postgraduate Diploma in Marketing. Paul is a qualified project and programme manager and is a practitioner in both PRINCE2 and MSP.

With a 30 year career in high-tech engineering Paul project managed the development of the world's first Bluetooth solution, the custom CPU in the world's first internet enabled smartphone and the world's lowest power GPS solution. Paul is a Black Belt in Karate and former President of Oxford Speakers Club. Today Paul speaks, consults, trains and mentors high-growth companies. As well as specialising in business strategy Paul provides hands-on interim project and programme management services enabling a company's vision to become a predictable reality.

Special offer for *Breaking the Barriers to Business Growth* readers:
In the chapter, 'Creating Business Success through Strategy' I introduced an eight point framework that you as a modern-day entrepreneur can use to systematically build your business. This framework outlines eight key skill areas, which when mastered, can catapult your business to new heights.

By claiming your copy of a Special Report outlining this framework you can get deeper insight into the critical skill areas that you need to master in order to grow your business. You will also learn how the eight skill areas are inter-related and can reinforce each other. By mastering and putting into practice these enhanced skills you will be able to expand your business to progressively new levels. Being able to run circles around your competition is both fun and profitable!

Claim your copy now at: www.strategy2profits.com/growthstrategy

Chapter 2

The price is right?

Albert Wright

The price is right?
Albert Wright

Is there such a thing as the "right price" for a particular product or service?

Do entrepreneurs always have the power to control prices in every market?

This chapter is designed to get you thinking about prices and markets for your goods and services and how being in the wrong market or selling at the wrong price can be a barrier to business growth.

Some people think there is a "right price" they should pay, or at least think there should be, as many people fear being "ripped off" and want to be "protected".

In a pluralist economy such as the UK, I don't think the concept of the "right price", which in practice means a fixed selling price to the public from all suppliers/sellers of the same product or service, is likely to be very useful or get us very far when considering the wider idea of "price" in the market place.

However, there are several markets in which prices are actually "fixed", or appear to be "fixed", and markets where the price for certain products supplied by a variety of suppliers seems to be around the same level. It's not surprising, therefore, to hear customers talk of the "right" price.

In other markets the situation looks very different and the price of the same or similar products or services can be very different. Consumers who end up paying higher prices in these markets are sometimes happy to do so but at other times they can be left feeling that they have been taken advantage of.

What are the factors that affect price? Are prices fixed by the market or by entrepreneurs?

Traditional economic and conservative thinking declares that markets rule and prices are fixed by supply and demand and that over time a market price will emerge. Whilst there is still a fundamental truth to this argument, most markets today are far removed from a "perfect market" situation and as a result many more factors are involved in determining prices.

Entrepreneurs should think carefully about the market place they propose to enter and how prices have come to be set in that market. Markets with fixed prices are generally ones in which there are major barriers to business growth.

Morality, economics and prices

People can get very emotional about prices, particularly in stressful and unusual situations. After a natural disaster like a flood or an earthquake, most people think it is wrong for shopkeepers to charge higher prices for water and food that may be in short supply, yet from an economic point of view we know that scarcity will affect price and the price going up is a way that markets respond to bring about an increase in supply, which in time will cause prices to fall again.

Economics describes what is likely to happen and why, it does not make judgements.

In a book about Breaking the Barriers to Business Growth, I am not going to dwell on issues of morality. This is not to say people should not take a "moral" view and in another context I would be happy to explore issues of fairness and justice related to pricing, a perfectly legitimate subject, but as this is more a matter for philosophers and governments than for business owners, the "moral" aspect of price will not be covered here.

Marketing strategy before pricing strategy

Whatever business sector you may be in, before looking at your pricing strategy, you need to decide on your business and marketing strategies and understand where you have positioned yourself in the market.

Are you going for a "no frills" Easy Jet approach, the mass and mid-market of Tesco or the top end of the range like Rolls Royce and Bentley cars?

What will be the factors that differentiate you from your competitors; speed of response, quality of goods and services, range, availability, exclusiveness, after sales service, delivery, value, location, strength of guarantee.....?

A major area of decision relates to "range". You must decide if you are going to:

- try and cover one/a small number of products or services across a wide range of prices.

- have a wide range of products over a wide range of prices.

- have a wide or narrow range of products within a small price range.

Price range

Wide Price Range Narrow Product Range	Wide Price Range Wide Product Range
Narrow Price Range Narrow Product Range	Wide Product Range Narrow Price Range

Product range

Where you position yourself in terms of price and range will directly impact on the image you are trying to create and indirectly influence the way you might use the price factor to increase profits.

In general, a narrow product range around a narrow price range may enable you to buy particular products in bulk and take advantage of bulk discounts on purchases and offer good value for your target segment customers, as is done by John Lewis department stores.

A narrow price range at a high price level may be designed to attract only a particular group of customers, an approach which lies behind the concept of 5 Star hotels.

A narrow price range at a low price level combined with a narrow product range could define you as a discount food retailer like Aldi, while a quality butcher may focus on a wide product range over a narrow price range at the top of the market.

Having made a decision on where in the market you want to position yourself in terms of product range and price range, it's time to look a little deeper at pricing.

To start, let's look at fixed prices.

Fixed prices

Fixed selling prices fixed by the state

Fixed prices fixed by the state are generally associated with communist regimes like Soviet Russia, that had central state planning and rigid business practices designed to deliver a society in which people would get what they needed at the same price for everybody, since everyone would also be paid pretty much the same for working, as wages were also set by the state.

In the UK today the range of goods and services, where price is fixed by the state, is quite narrow and almost totally restricted to goods created and sold by the state such as licences and permits. This includes things like road fund licenses (tax discs), TV licences, birth/marriage certificates and passports, where sales are restricted to certain outlets, such as Post Offices or places authorised for services.

At the next level there are postage stamps with a specific face value sold at the same price by a wider range of outlets, with probably each making the same gross margin.

Then there are things like MOT certificates, available only from specific, registered garages, performing an identical "test" on motor vehicles, with common test criteria related to "Pass" or "Fail" with a maximum price set by the Government for the service.

Such fixed price only markets are generally avoided by entrepreneurs.

However, some suppliers will discount the price to the customer who wants their car tested to attract more or specific customers, with the intention of being able to supply any rectification work if the car fails the test.

In a similar way there are controlled prices/fees paid by the Government to licensed providers of services such as legal advice, paid for by the state but free at the point of use to some people/customers/clients.

We will spend no further time on this area of pricing where there is a "monopoly" supplier fixing prices, as there is little an entrepreneur can do about the prices involved.

The only way to increase profits is to cut costs and/or increase volume supplied (assuming the business is profitable).

Fixed selling prices fixed by sellers

Technically this is now illegal, following the abolition of Retail Price Maintenance back in the 1950s. Since then governments have been on a "competition" agenda to free up markets and prevent suppliers from controlling the final price to the consumer.

From time to time we read about prosecutions by the Price Commission or Office of Fair Trading against suppliers who collude together to set/control common prices (usually to prevent them from falling).

In recent years examples include suppliers of asphalt roofing products (particularly on tendered local government projects) and consumer air flight tickets on restricted travel routes.

Collusion can be profitable if it is kept secret. As it is illegal and the chances of being caught are relatively high and the penalties for breaking the law are potentially very high, we would not recommend this as a good way to increase profits.

Fixed selling prices fixed by the theory of market economics

This covers markets where a range of suppliers are offering almost identical products such as petrol fuel or diesel for cars to the general public through petrol stations.

Prices in these markets generally contain a large element of government imposed tax or duty leaving suppliers with little chance of affecting the final consumer price through better buying or major operational efficiencies.

Similar situations exist for branded tobacco and alcohol products.

It also covers fruit and vegetable/produce type markets, where several stalls are virtually side by side in a small geographic area and have very similar operating costs and sell short shelf life products such as bananas (in particular), imported by a small number of organisations.

The situation is similar, outside the English growing season, for lettuce, tomatoes and most short life salad products.

As the final seller to the public can do little to get a better buying-in price for the product and there is little room to get a lower operating cost by improving operational efficiency or lower premises costs – the market dictated prices are likely to be the same or similar, where little product or service differentiation can be introduced to what is a "commodity" product.

Almost fixed selling prices fixed by real markets

There is a growing trend among multiple food retailers, when selling high volume branded products (and sometimes own label) to highlight the prices in competitors' shops as being the same as theirs, in an attempt to dissuade customers going elsewhere to save a penny.

There is also often limited or no price differences in the motor trade from manufacturer licensed garages selling the same model. (The EU has special rules for this sector on pricing that result in little, if any, price competition).

The same is true with prices for products and services that lend themselves to price comparison on product price comparison web sites. The range is ever expanding and currently includes many electrical/white goods, branded clothing, car, house and contents insurance, branded flights and holidays, hotel rooms, vehicle hire, currency exchange, books and CDs/DVDs, software for PCs, electrical, electronic, digital gadgets etc.

This sector is expanding in range and value as a result of increased usage of the internet and on line selling, which provides increased information for buyers who take the trouble to look and search.

Technology has made "shopping around" easier for consumers for many products and services, which in turn has led to many retailers/suppliers offering "Price Guarantees" along the lines of John Lewis – "Never Knowingly Undersold".

With already tight margins in the retail sector and rising costs, this is not currently leading to a price war as No One Dares, since No One Knows (in advance) Who is Likely to Win.

Unless you are the lowest cost supplier and believe you will remain so, we would not recommend you enter this type of market place if you have a choice, as it will be difficult to raise profitability.

Summary

There are situations and circumstances where, for particular products and services, in certain locations, at certain times, in specific conditions (and in some cases, all circumstances and conditions) the price is more or less "fixed" and sellers have little choice in what they charge.

In such circumstances the businesses most likely to succeed are those with the lowest cost bases, as they will be the ones making the most/any profit.

If you choose to operate in such markets you need to ensure that your cost base allows you to make money at the prevailing prices, or, at the very least, not to make a loss.

Where the "fixed price" situation exists, but is only one part of your operation, even if you are making a loss on the "fixed price" element, it may still make sense to continue the activity. Many garages offer MOTs at a loss but cross subsidise this activity as a way of attracting customers who might fail the test but go on to have remedial work done by the garage at an overall profit to the garage.

Equally, if operating in a "fixed price" sector and wanting to make additional profits you might consider introducing additional products and services at higher gross margins, as many petrol stations do, by selling confectionery, food and drink, car washes etc from the same premises/site.

Whichever approach you take, you do need to do your sums, calculate your numbers and make sure you are earning a satisfactory mixed gross profit margin to at least cover your overheads and break even.

Albert S Wright BA
Expertise Focus: Pricing, Costing and Profit
Improvement

Albert is Managing Director of Millionaire Coaching
Academy Ltd (MCA), Small Business Solutions Ltd
(SBS), a partner in Right Angle Consultants (RAC)
and a Group Director for NABO Networking.

MCA develops and delivers mentoring and business
support programmes to accelerate the sales and
profits of small businesses from sales of around
£350,000 pa to £1,000, 000 pa within 24 months.
Where required, support continues on to further success with business
valuations of £1 million and later the extraction of £1m from the business for
private use. MCA's team of Millionaire Mentors have a track record in such
work and provide individually tailored programmes for each client.

SBS supports ambitious micro business owners with over two years of trading
experience to grow their sales and profits to specific levels in a given time by
providing training, coaching and "hands on" help.

The main role of RAC is to bring together the skills and experience of over
15 business specialists to provide training, consultancy and business support
materials to the SME market.

Albert has been active in the business support sector for over 20 years and
is licensed to deliver proven programmes including Accelerated Business
Growth (ABG) The Outstanding Professional (TOP), coaching via the
Coaching Academy and marketing support based on Rapid Results
techniques and templates.

Albert is a member of the Institute of Directors (IOD), Business Network
International (BNI), the Nationwide Alliance of Business Owners and NRG.
SBS belongs to the Federation of Small Businesses (FSB) and the National
Enterprise Network (NEN).

Special offer for *Breaking the Barriers to Business Growth* **readers:**
A FREE copy of Albert's printed book *Business Wisdom* normally sold for £17.
Claim your copy now at: www.businesswisdom.com

Chapter 3

Knowing the numbers: management accounts made manageable

Anthony Pilkington

Knowing the numbers: management accounts made manageable

Anthony Pilkington

This chapter aims to encourage the production and use of management accounts to improve business success.

What are management accounts?

Everybody has heard of management accounts, so everybody knows what they are. Well no, it's probably the opposite, so let's start with some explanation.

Management accounts are financial reports produced for the business owners and managers, generally monthly or quarterly, normally a Profit & Loss report and a Balance Sheet. In principle they are similar to Year End accounts but are less formal and personalised to the reader's requirements.

Who produces management accounts?

There are 4½ million businesses in the UK. A surprising 98% have 20 or fewer staff, 95% have 10 or fewer and 72% are just 1 person. Only a tiny fraction of these 98% have management accounts.

Why do so few businesses have management accounts?

There is a mixture of reasons:

- lack of interest
- never properly considered
- too small
- thought to be too small (but are not)
- just never started
- no formal accounting system
- assumed insufficient or inadequate in-house skill
- worried about the complexity

- perceived as unnecessary

- assumed unaffordable

- another job to do – too busy

It's fair to say that there will be some businesses that are truly too small or too simple to require detailed management accounts. However they will still benefit from at least a basic, quarterly summary of some sort and comparison with previous periods. It's a matter of opinion but arguable that turnover of £100,000 is not too small to benefit from some detail.

What most businesses do and the result

The norm is that no management accounts are produced and never have been. Most businesses have insufficient systems in place to know their true financial performance – if they did then they would have a starting point, rather than just assumptions which are often wrong. For example an Estate Agent with offices in three towns – when asked what the ranking of profitability was between the offices the two owners had no information. They put their heads together to estimate the ranking. In due course proper management accounts proved them completely wrong, yet they thought they were smart operators.

Typically a business measures its sales, knows its order book and might have an idea of the bank situation. But that's about all. It doesn't know its profitability or lack of it. It doesn't know which parts of the business are better than others – it just guesses or perhaps not even that. It doesn't know its overhead costs and doesn't compare performance month to month with previous years. It's woefully short of even basic financial information. Some businesses worry about this, others don't, but it stands to reason that if it's measured it can be improved. When all's said and done, that's what it's all about – the bottom line net profit.

The result is that the business under achieves profit or is taken by surprise because difficult circumstances can arise without warning, in particular shortage of cash and liquidity. Most businesses end up taking financial decisions in the dark and that can't be good. Without sound financial information the business is at risk of significant or serious underachievement in either profit or cash or both.

Another key effect of no accounts is the risk of overtrading – that is expanding sales too quickly so that the company runs out cash or working capital. In short, customers may not have paid before suppliers and staff demand their money. This is a very common reason for firms going bust and it's usually a huge surprise to the business owners. Proper financial information would highlight this happening so that corrective action could be taken before it's too late.

Even if management accounts are produced they may be failing to highlight vital information e.g. a £4 million consultancy with 19 projects – the problem here was that although the overall picture of the business was measured there was no split between the projects. The company had no idea of the profitability and lacked any financial control of individual projects.

Who uses management accounts?

- owners/managers
- investors
- banks/lenders
- factoring/invoice discounting
- accountants
- tax planners

Why produce them?

Running a business without management accounts is like driving a car in the dark. You know what speed you are doing from the wind noise and vibrations (your sales) but you don't know your direction (your profitability) and you can't see obstacles you are about to hit (shortage of cash & liquidity).

Most businesses don't know their profitability, margins and trends. So why bother? It's a fundamental principle that if you can measure it you can improve it, so assuming you want to increase your net profit it's rather a 'no brainer'.

There are several key objectives in financial reporting:

- To measure past performance as a basis for improving

- To avoid cashflow problems and manage liquidity

- To have future visibility

- To determine where to focus attention in order to improve profitability

Some specific reasons for producing management accounts:

- Measure the gross margin percentage. Broadly this is the gross profit (sales less direct costs) you make from your service or product divided by the sales value, excluding VAT. Armed with this information you can check your performance against others in your business sector. You can check trends over time and you are then in a position to take action to improve your profits

- It imposes a discipline of controlling the finances and may uncover bad practices

- It will tend to reduce year end accountants' costs as the information will be better and more likely to be reconciled

- Establish your breakeven point for profitable sales

- Check and control overhead costs

- Control stock levels – measure trends, benchmark it

- Control debtors – measure trends, benchmark it

- Manage the working capital cycle – changing stock, debtors and creditors affecting the bank position

- Use key performance indicators (KPIs) to see at a glance what's happening

Gross margin percentage

Most businesses do not know this information but it's really important to measure this accurately. Suppose you sell £500,000 per annum. If you can increase your margin by 1% your net profit will increase by £5,000. What is so beneficial is to check the margin as follows:

Check the trend over time – establish why it has changed, either up or down. Examine every part of the margin i.e. sales and direct costs to see what can be improved such as cutting out loss making sales, increasing sales to profitable customers etc.

Examine it like a hawk as soon as it's known each month – why has it changed?

Benchmark against comparable businesses in your sector – how well are you doing, should you be improving?

Marketing for profit using management accounts

Suppose you sell £2,000 of product in a month and your direct cost is £1,200, your gross profit is £800 which is a gross margin of 40%. To improve profits the tendency is to focus on sales. A 10% increase in sales will generate £80 more profit but a 10% increase in margin to 44% would increase profits by the same amount without the significant effort required to increase sales. To put it another way if the margin dropped to 36% you would have to increase sales by 10% to stand still. But if you don't have management accounts you cannot know what is happening to your margins. Thus without management accounts it is difficult to optimise profitability.

Once you know your gross margin as a percentage of sales you have the knowledge to experiment with price changes as part of your marketing mix, without the danger of going bust because your margin is wrong. If sales are not too good, many business owners think the best thing to do is trade their way out of the problem by reducing prices to win more sales. In many cases this is the worst thing to do, as it often has a negative effect on profits. Management accounts may show that increasing prices could be the better option. Take the following scenario.

For a product selling for £10 with a gross margin of 25%, reducing your price by 10% to £9 means you have to sell 66% more to make the same profit as before, (£2.50), yet increasing your price by £1 to £11 means you can afford to sell almost 30% less units and still make as much profit. The route to increased profits can often be through price increases, rather than price reductions.

Sale units	Sale each	Cost each	GP each	GP total
100	10	7.5	2.5	£250
166	9	7.5	1.5	£249
70	11	7.5	3.5	£245

Which is more likely to happen, price up by £1 per unit and sales fall by 30 units or less or price down by £1 per unit and sales up by 66 units or more?

How are management accounts produced?

The first requirement is a sound accounting system. This need not be complicated but it needs to be sound. This might be Sage or even just Excel, but whatever it is someone who knows what they are talking about should check its soundness. It's a matter of opinion as to who is capable, but a qualified accountant would be a good starting point. This need not cost a lot, sometimes it's free but it's an essential one-off check because if your accounts are unsound then you will produce unsound or misleading reports and hence you may make wrong decisions.

Armed with sound information it's then quite straightforward to design reports to your requirements, even for a small business with modest accounting skills. You might need help but it will probably be worth the investment.

What skills are required to produce management accounts?

This is a bit tricky to answer because to a certain extent it depends on what they are being used for but generally the book-keeper, with possible assistance at a month end, needs to be capable of covering the following:

A bank reconciliation – absolutely essential, you must prove that you have this and not assume anything. If in doubt check with your accountant, it's a 10 minute job.

- Reconciliation of VAT – usually not done
- Reconciliation of PAYE & wages – usually not done
- Sound up to date sales ledger i.e. debtor information
- Sound up to date purchase ledger i.e. creditor information
- Stock and work in progress if your business has changing values
- Accruals & prepayments – usually not done
- Depreciation

But beware – only top book-keepers achieve all of the above so take very special care when recruiting as you will be putting all your trust in this one person. Thoroughly check references and find someone to check their skills, perhaps your accountant. What you are looking for is a reconciler, not just an input clerk.

What do management accounts look like?

They can be produced from your accounting system such as Sage or in Excel. Sage is rather basic but at least a good starting point. Check that the chart of accounts is sound i.e. not missing any accounts or duplicating accounts.

Excel is more flexible but it's important to reconcile to your accounting system (unless that is just Excel) otherwise you may show wrong information which rather defeats the objective.

If your accounting system is just Excel and you have just a cash book summary then ensure that this reconciles to your bank account. You should also realise that this would be purely a cash picture, which is not the same as a profit & loss. Profit & loss is a measure of performance over an accounting period, whereas the cash position is a snapshot picture of cash balances at a specific point in time.

Ideally your reports will include budgets so you can compare against your target. What do you expect for sales, gross margin %, overheads etc.?

Where the business can be split into sectors/departments/locations/projects then separate the reporting accordingly. The results are often surprising and will lead to effective profitable management action.

It's easy also to compare against previous years or even a number of years. What does the trend look like?

You can go below the surface and check your top performing customers and products – then aim to boost or replicate.

What to do with management accounts outside the business?

- Impress your bank with some facts, it's what they are normally desperately missing. It's best to report regularly, good or bad. In fact accompanying bad information with some commentary and plan to fix will be much appreciated, it will certainly mark you out from other businesses who simply don't report. You are much more likely to win a facility and at a better rate with quality MI (Management Information) as the banks say.

- Report to your investors – this will be really appreciated if not essential

- Issue to your factoring or invoice discounting provider

- Allow your accountants or part time Financial Director to advise on performance

- Allow your accountants to plan your tax affairs

- Use as a basis for obtaining more and lower cost facilities

Conclusion

Management accounts offer business owners the opportunity to gain critical insights into the financial side of business performance. They can give a 'dashboard' just like that a pilot needs to guide an aeroplane. On the one hand, management accounts can give early warning signs of negative trends, while on the other hand, the insights gained lead to better business decisions, which will allow you to optimise profitability. Naturally, higher profitability enables greater investment in the business and hence facilitates future growth.

Anthony Pilkington FCA
Expertise Focus: Book-keeping with management accounts

Anthony is Managing Director of BookCheck Ltd, a team developed since 1994. His company of 50 book-keepers goes on to produce management accounts, always both thoroughly checked and issued personally by a qualified accountant under ISO 9001 certification.

Anthony is a chartered accountant by training but now accountants are top referrers to BookCheck as it makes their year ends much more efficient and hence lower cost.

BookCheck sees daily the huge benefits in producing quality management accounts – even multi £million companies improve with better information. At the same time book-keeping is often a constant pain which the business could and should do without.

Special offer for *Breaking the Barriers to Business Growth* **readers:**

- Free 30 point HealthCheck of the book-keeping system, from a qualified accountant.

- Free survey of reporting Sage data in Excel, easily and powerfully.

- Free Top 20 Book-keeping Tips.

Contact

anthony.pilkington@bookcheck.co.uk

call 0800 026 6522

www.bookcheck.co.uk
@BookCheck_Ltd

Chapter 4

Growth is good but cash is better

Rob Warlow

Growth is good but cash is better
Rob Warlow

So you have managed to scrape through the toughest and mostly costly recession in living memory. You're still trading and now ready to enter a new growth phase. You have been prospecting, getting new and existing clients interested in your products again and then it all suddenly kicks in and the orders start flowing again. Wonderful! But is it?

Many business owners say that the greatest challenge they face in going for growth is tackling the sales and marketing jungle, but it's only when the hard work pays off do they realise they face an even bigger challenge ... cashflow.

Many businesses ultimately fail not because of lack of sales but because of a lack of cash, and growing companies are particularly vulnerable to falling into this trap.

Why is cashflow so important?

Cash is the lifeblood of your business. You can have a healthy order book but without cash flowing through your business it's all in vain.

Cash moves in a cycle. It has a starting point and it moves through a series of stages, sometimes quickly and sometimes slowly. The speed with which it moves through this cycle dictates the pace at which you can grow. Your cashflow position, and so your ability to fund growth, is down to the time lag between paying out and getting paid. It's as simple as that.

See the illustration below which shows the typical working capital cycle.

Stage one: cash, overdraft, creditors

The cycle starts with three sources of funding, being cash, bank overdraft or creditors. Cash in the bank is straightforward; a bank overdraft of say £50,000 is akin to cash in the bank; and finally there are your creditors, being your suppliers who will grant you say 60 days grace before you have to pay.

Stage two: stock, raw material

The next stage is the purchase of stock or raw materials. This is the first of the 'dead-money' stages – cash invested here earns nothing. Your aim is to keep cash tied up in this stage to a minimum. Your stock ordering process has to be lean and efficient. You cannot afford to over stock or stock a slow moving item. The longer cash is tied up in this phase the lower the amount available to fund stage three.

Stage three: work in progress

If you are in manufacturing, once you have started the production process your cash moves to Work in Progress (WIP). If you are in a service sector you have your investment tied up in the time you are working until you invoice.

Again, this is a dead-money stage. You may be adding value or building up billable hours, but it has no cash value. Your aim is to streamline your production process so you move to the next stage as quickly as possible.

Stage four: finished goods

In this stage your stock is ready to be delivered, or, if you're in the service sector, you're on the point of invoicing. To ensure you have as little cash as possible tied up, keep your stock of finished goods as to a minimum but of sufficient size to guarantee your ability to meet orders as they come in.

Stage five: debtors

The final stage is where cashflow problems usually arise – debtors. Even if you don't formally give a set number of days to pay, for example 30 or 60 days, you are still likely to have cash sitting here due to the time lag between when your invoice is sent out and the time you actually get paid.

This is where the importance of having an efficient debtor collection process or credit management policy in place comes to the fore. You cannot afford to have 30 days becoming 60 days. The key message is …

The longer cash is tied up in this final stage the less you have available to keep the cycle going.

If you can't turn your debtors back into cash quickly enough to replenish your cash position, reduce your overdraft or pay off creditors, then you won't have sufficient resources to start the cycle over again.

The working capital cycle

By following the stages of your working capital cycle you can see that a delay in any of the stop-off points can bring your business to a halt and this is the crux of a cashflow problem.

How cashflow can hold back your growth

When your working capital cycle is perfectly in sync, everything goes smoothly, the cash flows seamlessly from one stage to the next. The problem comes when there is a blockage in the system or an unexpected strain is placed on one of the processes, such as a growth spurt. This usually comes down to poor planning.

Let's assume you have been successful in obtaining a batch of new orders. You start off by looking at your available cash resources and all looks great, so you start investing by moving to stage two of the cycle.

What you may not realise is that the resources needed to fund each stage are now larger – looking at the Working Capital Cycle model you can imagine that each bubble is now larger to reflect the increased cash tied up in each stage.

Eventually you get to the fifth stage where cash is tied up in debtors. Here, your limited cash resources (limited because you tapped into the headroom you had available in the first place) are now trapped; you have a larger amount invested in debtors than you previously had. Assuming that your business is now back on a growth path you'll find that, with a larger amount lodged in the debtors bubble, you don't have sufficient resources in stage one (cash, bank or creditor terms) to keep the cycle going. Slowly your business grinds to a halt.

This is the essence of an unplanned for, growth-fuelled, cashflow crisis – insufficient resources being made available to keep the working capital cycle in sync.

How to plan for successful growth

As with all aspects of running a successful business, managing growth is down to effective planning and preparation.

The first step is to prepare a cashflow forecast which will highlight the impact of your growth plans on your cash position and requirement. You already know the terms you are getting from your suppliers, how long it takes to get your goods or services to invoice stage and the terms granted to your clients for payment, so you have the basis on which to prepare a cashflow forecast.

If you are well outside your comfort zone talk to your accountant, business adviser, mentor or coach but it's vital you don't miss out on this exercise. It's crucial you understand how much additional cash you are going to need to fund your growth plans.

If your projections indicate that you will need additional cash, or equivalent resources, here are steps you can take to ensure your growth plans are not tripped up by a hiccup in cashflow.

Speak to your cash resource suppliers

Your first port of call is to speak to your bank for an increase in borrowing facilities or to approach your creditors to request an extension in terms.

Alternatively you can inject the additional capital required. If none of these is an option, or you have been refused support, then consider other options to speed up the cycle.

Examine your processes

Are you as efficient as you could be in stages two to four? Could you improve your production process, your handling of WIP, and how quickly your finished goods are moved on? A small revision in your processes may release the cash you need.

Squeeze your debtor portfolio

Cash can be released by increasing the speed that the debtors in stage five are turned into cash. If your client leverage is strong you can reduce your credit terms from say 60 days to 45 days. Alternatively you can consider factoring or entering into an invoice discounting arrangement, which will allow you to access the cash tied up almost immediately upon invoice.

Other strategies to improve cashflow

Here are some other ways to speed up the movement of cash:

- Invoice more quickly – if you wait until month end to invoice think about moving to twice a month or as an order is completed

- Ask for a percentage of order value up front – this will give you an immediate cash boost

- Offer an early settlement discount – this will hurt your margin but may provide a much needed cash injection

- Don't Do Nothing!

You can see that aiming for growth in an ad-hoc manner can cause chaos. Uncontrolled growth should be seen as part of a larger strategic problem … lack of planning.

Don't unwittingly putting your business at risk by not planning ahead and so being ignorant of the wider implications.

Plan early and plan for success.

Rob Warlow
Expertise Focus: Business Finance, Planning and Strategy

Rob Warlow started out in banking in 1984 with Barclays Bank PLC where over the years he held a number of junior and senior positions. In 1999 he left the UK to take up a position in Uganda heading up the bank's corporate team where he stayed for 2 years. In 2001 he moved again with Barclays to Mauritius to take up the post of Risk Management Director. Having got a taste for life as an expatriate in 2003 Rob left Barclays and returned to Uganda as Managing Director of a private-owned bank. Three years later he joined a bank in Kenya leaving in late 2009 as the Group CEO overseeing operations in 3 East African countries.

In December 2009, after spending 25 years in banking in the UK and Africa, Rob returned to the UK to set-up Business Loan Services. Using his extensive banking knowledge he now helps small and medium-sized businesses to develop, grow and access bank finance. In assisting business owners raise development funding, whether that be debt or equity, Rob's focus is to look beyond the need and spot the issues which can delay or prevent the necessary funding being obtained.

Rob is also an accomplished public speaker sharing his ideas and thoughts on accessing finance and dealing with growth to business owners and groups across the UK. Rob is the author of *Loan Sharp: Get the Business Finance You Deserve*, which is a self-help guide for business owners on what banks are looking for when assessing a request for finance. You can find 'Loan Sharp' in all good bookshops and major online stores.

For more details on Rob's services and how to contact him visit www.businessloanservices.co.uk

Special offer for *Breaking the Barriers to Business Growth* readers:
During Rob's time in dealing with businesses of all sizes he has found that there are a common set of reasons as to why businesses fail. To find out what they are send Rob an email at info@businessloanservices.co.uk and claim your free report, '10 Reasons Why Small Businesses Fail and How to Avoid Being One of Them'.

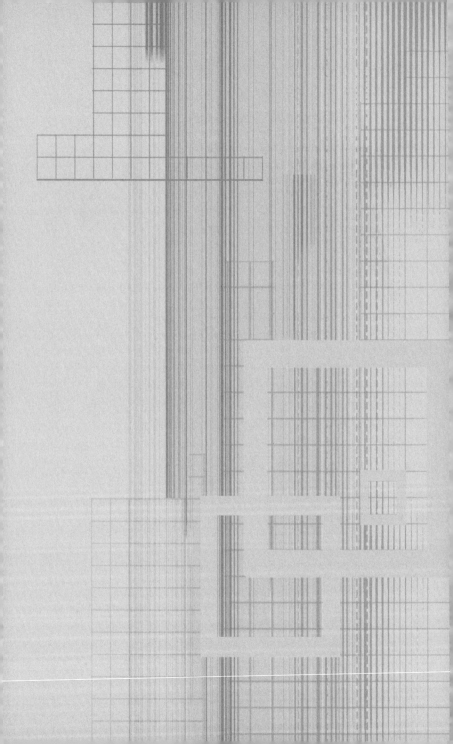

Chapter 5

Think Brand
not bland

Phil Strachan

Think Brand not bland
Phil Strachan

The importance of thinking Brand not bland

Let's face it, not every business can expect to be a Coca Cola, a Nike, an Apple, a L'Oréal, a Google, a Virgin, a Harley Davidson or an Armani overnight. However, every business owner, whatever size their business, can learn from what made these stand-out businesses successful by understanding what it is that they have in common and by applying this learning.

One thing for certain is that none of these successful businesses could reasonably be described as bland. They are all most certainly brands rather than blands. They are iconic brands rather than just businesses – they stand out from the crowd, they are individual, they have personality and character in abundance and they all represent a promise consistently delivered. They deliver real value, substantial added value, both to their target markets and to their owners and shareholders alike. That is what the highly successful businesses listed above have done, and continue to do, so well.

The concept of brands representing perceived added value must not be underestimated because that is precisely why people choose to select and buy brands rather than products. Added value clearly represents benefit to the consumer or customer and more profit potential to businesses. Yet why is it, when I am about to address an audience of SME business owners on the subject of brands and branding, I am often told something like "Oh, I'm not a Coca Cola, this will not be relevant to me" or "It is just me, I am not a brand" or "I can't afford to spend the money to create a brand".

Furthermore, when I ask these same business people to raise their hands if they have a brand, maybe only 15 to 20 % raise their hands with any conviction (most often those running branded franchises!) and a further 10 to 15% hesitantly, uncertainly and almost apologetically raise their hands only part way.

What these audiences clearly do not understand is that they are brands, they are already brands, whether they like it or not and whether they have deliberately set out to create a brand or not. They may not be a good brand, they may not be the brand that they would like to be, but they are brands nonetheless. They already have a brand image and they are being judged on that image. What they have to decide is whether or not they wish to be in control of that image.

Seeing is believing

 It is vitally important to understand that brands exist only in the hearts and minds of their existing and target consumers and customers. They are not 'real', they don't really exist. They are simply the sum total of all the tangible and intangible, rational and emotional associations and experiences built up over time.

What really matters is how your business is perceived, which is not necessarily the same as the way in which you think it should be perceived or want it to be perceived, at each and every consumer or customer touchpoint. In the world of brands, perception equals reality. For example, if your business is perceived to be slow at responding to consumer or customer enquiries, your business might be branded as inefficient at best and uninterested and rude at worst. Whatever the case, you are likely to lose out to a competitor who is perceived and believed to be more efficient, hungrier and likely to offer better customer service, ie to offer a better brand experience. That is why I believe that branding is fundamentally the art of managing perceptions.

Differentiation, differentiation, differentiation

Importantly, while much can be learned from the businesses and brands that get it right, there is just as much, if not more, to be learned from the businesses and brands that don't get it right.

The brand of a business is what separates and differentiates it from its competitors and prevents it from being lost in the crowd in a sea of sameness. Unless seen to stand for something in particular, your business might be in danger of being seen to stand for nothing in particular and therefore to represent no discernable added value.

If you are to be successful in growing your business, if you are to survive and thrive in today's recession and emerge successfully from it, you need to do everything possible to differentiate your business positively from your competitors. That requires knowing what it is that makes you different and better, combined with the ability to connect, communicate and engage successfully and consistently with your identified target market.

Clearly, there is a choice. You can choose to go for bland differentiation or brand differentiation. However, if you are looking to grow your business, there is no choice because the message has to be to think brand not bland. It is very simple. Do you want to be seen as a distinctive brand or distinctly bland, a non-entity or a well-known entity? It really is your choice and within your power.

If you think about it, we live in a world in which we are surrounded by brands. There are brands everywhere we look and everywhere we go – from retail brands, to product brands, to service brands. We ourselves constantly choose and buy brands, whether in the Supermarket, the DIY store or the Off Licence (and we probably made a deliberate brand choice about where to shop) and we select and buy brands when it comes to clothing, cars, insurances or sporting goods. Why then should we think that our consumers and/or customers will not be choosing to buy brands when it comes to the products and services that we offer? After all, we do not want to buy generic, me-too commodities – we want to buy brands that we can relate to, brands that we can identify with. We do not want to buy bland – so, why should our consumers or customers?

The simple fact of life is that there is no point in being a bland – the default brand bland – you need to think brand if you are serious about creating a business with serious growth potential. In fact, your greatest barrier to growth could be your own thinking, so break down this barrier and think brand not bland.

Just another anonymous blot on the blandscape

What can be gained by being seen to be just AN Other solicitor, AN Other accountant, AN Other consultant, AN Other event organiser, AN Other business coach, AN Other website designer, etc.? If your business is not seen to be different, it will be seen to be the same, to lack character, to lack any distinguishing feature, to be devoid of any distinctive merit, to be unremarkable, unexciting, uninteresting, dull – in short, to be bland rather than brand.

If your business is simply seen as bland, as just another anonymous blot on the blandscape, this cannot possibly be a recipe for success in terms of building a successful business and driving business growth given the fact that consumers and customers choose brands over commodities.

What possible future can there be in being a corporate bland or having umbrella blands, product blands, service blands, FMCG blands, experiential blands, core blands or sub-blands all delivering truly forgettable bland experiences. There are plenty of bland brands out there already, plenty of blands masquerading as brands, for the simple reason that they are insufficiently differentiated from their competitors. Why be one of them? We have all come across them and many of them seem to be little more than wanton acts of brandalism, blands with delusions of blandeur and with very little hope and even less chance of any glory when it comes to growth potential and likelihood of survival.

There is surely absolutely nothing to be gained by having any kind of bland that is built on a bland platform, a bland positioning statement and a bland proposition. What good is bland integrity and bland alignment based on bland attributes and bland benefits? Precisely who is going to be wooed by a bland promise from a bland that is rich in bland personality and simply oozes bland character by the bucketful?

There can surely be no future in creating a bland portfolio comprising mega-blands, global blands, premium blands, power blands, luxury blands, drive blands, challenger blands, fighting blands and niche blands all with their own bland identities and at varying stages of their bland life cycles because at the end of the day they will all still be blands. And what possible reason could there be to conduct a re-blanding exercise when surely it would be preferable for today's underperforming bland to be transformed into one of tomorrow's top performing brands with the injection of some good solid brand thinking?

Similarly, it is completely pointless investing in bland innovation, bland evolution, bland building, bland stretching or bland extension programmes to leverage the bland. Bland in – bland out!

In the kingdom of the bland...

And, if you stop to think about it, who could possibly be interested in bland licensing, bland franchising or co-blanding opportunities that simply fail to connect, communicate and engage with their intended target markets? Who could possibly aspire to be guardian of the bland or head of bland marketing? Yet they seem to be out there, writing bland plans that are clearly the direct result of bland vision, a bland mission statement and the bland objectives they drove out in the first place. Nothing wrong with that providing that they are just looking to bland in and to create the bland that time forgot.

If you are a sole trader, there is little point in aspiring to be the bland leader in your market or market sector because that would surely just be a case of the bland leading the bland and in the kingdom of the bland the one-man bland will never be king even if he religiously follows a carefully constructed set of bland guidelines to ensure that he is, at all times, well and truly blanded.

Armed with all the tools of bland management at our disposal, it is clearly a very easy matter to come up with bland names that fail to register, bland identities that fail to connect, bland advertising campaigns that fail to communicate, bland packaging designs that are instantly forgettable and bland promotions that fail to engage. You hardly need to conduct a bland audit to realise that the result of such bland marketing would be unacceptable levels of bland awareness, bland recall, bland interaction, bland trial and bland loyalty.

There is little or no value in being bland. There are no iconic blands out there because almost by definition this would be a contradiction in terms – iconic brands do not run with the pack but rather break with convention in a manner that ensures that their target consumer or customer has something powerful and individual to identify with, to relate to. They are perceived to be unique. It hardly takes a genius to work out that if you combine bland equity with powerful bland values you can only reasonably expect a bland valuation – bland is bland and is not worth a lot to anyone.

Time to jump on the blandwagon?

So what is it to be? Do you just join the crowd, jump on the blandwagon and reach for the bland guidelines manual or do you elect to think brand not bland? Do you leave your brand to chance or take control of your own destiny?

Whether you are looking to create a new business or to take an established business to the next level, stop and think. Think Brand not bland. But don't just jump in, grab a name and get a quick and cheap logo done and believe that you will have created a successful brand or even the basis for one. A name and a logo are only brand identifiers to assist brand recognition. They are not the brand, they are only what stand for the brand, forms of shorthand for the brand. They are not what the brand stands for which is what consumers and customers value and buy.

Furthermore, you need to live the brand and deliver the brand at all times, as do any employees you may have. Whether they operate in sales, customer service or at the checkout, employees, whether full-time or part-time, need to have a clear understanding of your brand if they are to be effective brand ambassadors and play their part in delivering the required brand experience.

So, know your target market, know your competitors, know your USP and know what you want to be seen to stand for. Then think about how you will express and communicate that including what your business name and business identity will be in order take ownership of that and make it your own. That is what will set you apart and provide the platform for business growth and success because good branding can be truly transformational.

Take care to ensure that you are building your brand on a compelling brand promise and not on an empty bland promise – and make sure that you keep that promise because a successful brand is a contract and promise built on reputation and trust – and it has to be earned.

So, just do it, because you're worth it, be the real thing, be reassuringly expensive – THINK BRAND NOT BLAND.

Business
& Brand
Alchemy

Phil Strachan BA(Hons)
Expertise Focus: Branding, Identity,
Creativity, Innovation & Design

Trading as Strangebrew, Phil is a Business and Brand Alchemist who somewhat uniquely combines 15 years hands-on client side marketing management experience with blue chip companies and brands with 20 years experience on the branding, identity and design consultancy side.

In 1991, Phil set up QED (Quite Extraordinary Design) Partnership as the managing partner with two experienced designers and was instrumental in initiating and implementing the revitalisation/refreshment/relaunching of brands such as Foster's Lager (UK and Europe), Alpen, Pontin's, Monster Munch, Warres Port, Jose Cuervo and Baxters Soups and delivering many and varied projects including the merchandising and promotion of brands such as Dulux and Hugo Boss.

Today, as the founder of Strangebrew, Phil adds real value to and creates real advantage for businesses and brands of all shapes and sizes. His very varied clients range from one person start-ups through to established blue chip multinationals where he is still regularly called upon to deliver projects involving global premium brands.

With an ability to quickly distil the essence of a business or brand and to identify what makes it different, Phil uses his well practised blend of strategic and creative skills to deliver effective and affordable solutions to help them to think and be brand – not bland.

Special offer for *Breaking the Barriers of Business Growth* **readers:**
As a Scotsman living south of the border since 1975, it has been observed that Phil can justifiably make the claim that he consistently delivers 'London quality at Glasgow prices'. Phil is happy to offer his time for a one hour 'no cost and no strings attached' clinic to anyone who would like to take advantage of an appraisal of the presentation of their business and/or brand(s) and get a taste for what an injection of business and brand alchemy could do for them. To take advantage of this offer, please register your interest at www.thinkbrandnotbland.co.uk/freeclinic

Chapter 6

Finders and keepers: communicating with your customers in words that work for them

Sarah Williams

Finders and keepers: communicating with your customers in words that work for them

Sarah Williams

The game has changed, suddenly, radically, and for ever. Where once you knew your customers face to face, and could chat with them over the counter or in the street, now your customers could be, literally, anywhere.

Some quick statistics up front, guaranteed to simultaneously chill your blood and make your heart race with the possibilities for ever greater growth:

World regions	Population (est. 2010)	Internet users latest data	Pene-tration (% of pop.)	Growth 200-2010	Users % of table
Africa	1,013,779,050	110,931,700	10.9%	2,357.3%	5.6%
Asia	3,834,792,852	825,094,396	21.5%	621.8%	42%
Europe	813,319,511	475,069,448	58.4%	352%	24.2%
Middle East	212,336,924	63,240,946	29.8%	1,825.3%	3.2%
North America	344,124,450	266,224,500	77.4%	146.3%	13.5%
Latin America/ Caribbean	592,556,972	204,689,836	34.5%	1,032.8%	10.4%
Oceania/ Australia	34,700,201	21,263,990	61.3%	179.0%	1.1%
WORLD TOTAL	6,845,609,960	1,966,514,816	28.7%	444.8%	100.0%

Statistics of internet usage per head of population as at April 2010

Almost independently of what your product or service is, and what your conventional markets have been, you can now have customers and potential customers from Birmingham to Beijing, from Cardiff to Kolkata. And, of course, where there are potential customers, there are also potential competitors...

That's the broader context in which you're operating today – a world in which more people are more accessible more quickly than ever before.

What about the narrower context – the context of you and your business? You already have, or are looking to have, a high-growth business. And you are looking to survive the challenges that you know rapid growth can bring, so that your business, and you, will emerge the other side of the 'growth barrier' robust, resilient and ready for anything.

So, fundamentally, you are facing not one but two growth challenges: the perennial challenge of keeping everything together while your business is exploding around you, where the systems and strategies that brought you this far simply won't do any more, and the radical new challenge of the global game-changer that is the internet.

You have three choices when faced with surviving and thriving in this newly dynamic environment.

You can pretend it's not happening…

You can panic…

You can prepare yourself properly and start your ascent…

As you're reading this book, we'll assume you've gone for option 3.

What preparations can you make, then, in terms of company communications, which will enable you to climb safely and reach the heights, while not getting blown off the mountain by the gusting winds of change or slipping back down through a failure in your equipment?

Let's start with what you can do in terms of where your company is now, to confirm and consolidate those things which have already brought you success and to make sure that you don't lose track of what has already worked while you take on new systems and strategies.

From there we can move on to looking at the global situation, and how you can best extend your established good habits into your communications on the world wide web.

Stage 1: Where you are now

It's probably worth your while having a notebook, a sheet of paper or your laptop by your side for this next bit, as I'm going to be asking you a few questions just to help you orientate yourself, and to help you triangulate exactly where you are. As with anything in life, it's only when you know where you are that you can safely move forward.

Customer Inventory

Some very straightforward questions, but which don't always have very straightforward answers. I'm going to skip over these in a fairly speedy fashion, because they are dealt with more extensively in other chapters of this book, but fundamentally I would just like to ask you to note down who were or are:

- your core past customers and what they bought from you;

- your repeat customers and what they buy from you;

- your target customers and what you want them to buy from you.

Now make a note in as much detail as can of the characteristics of each of these groups – whether they are male or female, old or young, wealthy or waged, if they're retired or in work, and, if they're in work, what work they are doing. Even if you are selling to large corporates, you are still dealing with individual human beings – who are they, what are they like? The more you can segment your customer base, and identify its profile, the more successful your communications will be.

Communications Inventory

Now let's look in detail at how you currently communicate with people. For the moment we're going to leave internal company communications to one side, though they're crucially important too. However, given constraints of time and space, we'll deal here with how you communicate with your customers, past, current and to come.

Have a look through the table below, and work out which of these you do. If you like, you can fill in the grid as you go along.

Mode of communication	Often	Sometimes	Never
Networking (face to face)			
Flyers			
Advertisements			
Advertorials			
Brochures			
Cards			
Mailshots			
Cold calling (telephone)			
Website(s)			
Newsletters (print)			
Newsletters (email)			
Facebook			
Ecademy			
LinkedIn			
Twitter			

Ideally, you will already know which of these are the most successful in bringing you customers, and you will have worked out the return on investment on each of the channels which you use. And, of course, if you haven't, you need to start doing that right now. It's not always easy, and, as we'll see, communicating with your customers is about much more than just getting them to make a purchase, but you do need to have set some sort of metrics in place in terms of what you want each individual communication to achieve and a way of measuring whether or not it has done so. This is a crucial part of testing your climbing equipment, just like knowing what sort of terrain your boots are suitable for or what is the breaking strain of your rope.

Now, you already have customers, so you're already good at communicating with them. However, as your business grows, it becomes only too easy to forget what it was that worked about the ways in which you contacted your prospects and customers in the early days, and, even, more, it's almost inevitable that we start taking our past customers and our existing repeat customers for granted. You're so hard pressed simply dealing with what is happening every day, keeping the deliveries going, and meeting new demands, that it's easy to overlook the people and the purchases who have got you to where you are today.

It's an old truism in marketing that it's 7 times more expensive to acquire a new customer than it is to sell to an existing one. It is also a fundamental reality that there are only 24 hours in the day, and that you do need to sleep for at least a few of them. So, to keep your business growing and on track, to keep your existing customers on board as well as going after new ones, you're going to have to put some new systems in place.

Stage 2: Getting to where you want to be

You now have a list of all your customers, past, repeat and prospects, broken down into demographics, gender, age profiles and every other detail you feel may be relevant.

You already know what communications you put out at the moment and you have an idea (more or less accurate – but getting more refined day by day…) of which are the best performing for you and your business.

What I'd like to do now is to look in detail at the function of each of these communications and how they can be grouped together, organised and systematised. This is partly what any good CRM system will do, but I want to take you one step further, so that you are creating an entirely bespoke communications system, tailored to your business, your customers, and your mutual benefit.

Let us put to one side face to face and telephone communications, though these are important, and need to be brought consciously into the arena of how you present your business to the public, and how you address different individuals. For the time being, however, let us confine ourselves to written communications, and let us divide them into three main camps – those designed to build your brand, those designed to maintain contact, and those designed to sell stuff.

You will immediately see that you do far more brand building and maintaining contact than you do actual selling – and that is exactly as it should be. You build the brand, and that draws people to get in touch with you. Once they're in touch with you, you maintain contact with them. And once you've developed a relationship with them, you're in a position to sell to them.

What you need to do is to see this as a deliberate sequence, and set up a system to move people along from awareness to contact to action. But, as well as setting up a sequence of communications to be sent out at different times of the cycle, you also need to talk in importantly different ways at each of the stages of the cycle.

What does this mean in practice?

Brand building: As you will have seen in Chapter 5, defining and building your business brand is core to achieving and maintaining business success. The big corporates – Nike, Coca Cola, Disney – spend literally millions of dollars on building, developing and defending their brands. One of the key aspects of a brand is its 'personality', which should work in harmony both with what it is you are selling and with the values and outlooks of your core customers. Nike = sports, health, achievement. Coca Cola = fun, conviviality, youth. Disney = family, tradition, enjoyment. And so on.

What is the personality of your brand, and how does it connect with the visions and values of your customers? Are you selling an element in a cure for cancer to pharmaceutical companies? Then you'll want to be sober, reliable, knowledgeable, straight. Are you selling ice-cream to children? Then you'll want to be chatty, upbeat, fun. Are you selling executive training services to large corporates? Then you'll want to be clear, straightforward, imaginative and thoughtful. Partly this is conveyed by the imagery you choose, the colours you select, but most, and above all, it is conveyed by the language you use – and the language you use should be consistent throughout all your brand-building communications.

Keeping in contact: This is where the demographic breakdown of your customer profiles really comes into play. Assuming that you're writing in English, you have a whole toybox of language to choose from, from the very formal and traditional, usually Latin-based words, through the clear, direct words with Anglo-Saxon roots (give, take, have…), all the way through to the chatty and conversational (though I would caution against using slang – nothing dates faster and nothing marks you out more ruthlessly as a poser and a wannabe). There is a whole fascinating array of tools and weapons at your disposal when writing English. This is something I go into in far more depth in my book, *Are You Talking to Me? Getting the Language Right for Your Target Market.*

Selling: You have built up a relationship and developed rapport through the ways in which you have communicated with your customers. Now they trust you, and you can invite them to take action – usually this will mean moving from the formal or the chatty to the more direct. Directness denotes urgency, and you want your customers to take action urgently…

Stage 3: The global situation

All of the above holds true, only even more intensely when communicating on the internet, and the same division between brand-building, rapport-building and making sales is relevant.

There are two key things to remember, though, when writing for the net.

The first is that you don't know who is reading what you're writing, so you need to steer a careful middle course between drawing in those you want to attract and not driving away, through excessive formality or chattiness, those who might want to get to know you more. Generally, though, communications on the internet have a more relaxed and informal tone than many printed communications.

The second thing to remember is that you have an increasingly brief period of time in which to catch and keep a reader's attention. It's not just the 140 characters you're allowed on Twitter – it's the fact that the average visitor to a web page drops off after 7 seconds if they haven't found what they want. And even once they do hang around, they rarely read what you've written, they skim and scan, and click and flit. So don't write deathless, or even breathless prose, write headlines, bullet points, bite-sized chunks…

So you've got all your systems in place, your demographics are sorted, the language for each customer group and marketing channel set out in your company communications style guide – you're future proof and ready to roll…

Now that you've reached the top of the mountain, which peak are you going to conquer next?

Sarah Williams BA(Hons), MPhil, PGCE, MSA
Expertise Focus: Marketing communications and internal company communications

Sarah Williams has always been driven by a fascination with words, and how they can be made to work effectively. After a first degree at Sussex University, and a second degree in Comparative Literature, she started working as a professional writer, both as a book reviewer for the *Daily Telegraph*, the *Sunday Telegraph* and the *London Review of Books*, amongst others, and as a translator of non-fiction books from the French.

She worked as a tutor for the Open University before being asked to go and help run the English office of the largest French children's book publisher, and handle their spin-off English list. This is where Sarah cut her marketing teeth, and honed her craft as a writer, providing all the promotional material for all the books, as well as often providing original English text for them as well.

In due course, Sarah became a full time freelance writer, writing and editing textbooks and course books for English secondary schools (and some American high schools). Sarah has published well over 80 books under her writing name of Sarah Matthews.

In 2003, Sarah founded Wordsmith, a copywriting company, which has helped clients as large as e.on, as prestigious as The British Library and as specialised as HMRC with their internal and marketing communications, as well as providing effective online and offline marketing copy for hundreds of SMEs.

For more details about all Wordsmith can do, visit www.wordsmithtm.co.uk.

Special offer for *Breaking the Barriers to Business Growth* readers
How you communicate with your customers, your prospects, your team has an immediate effect on how they relate to you, react to you, work with you. Your complimentary copy of Sarah's e-book on the ways in which different people react to different kinds of language, *Are you Talking to Me?*, is available for you to download now from www.wordsmithtm.co.uk/rightwords. Worth £15.

Chapter 7

Use social media

Mary Thomas

Use social media
Mary Thomas

To achieve business growth, you need to make people aware of you and your business. One of the most cost effective and time efficient ways of talking to a large number of people is to use social media. In this chapter, we will discuss what we mean by social media and how to select the correct combination of social media tools dependent upon your aims, your audience, your business type, your content and your resources.

What is social media?

Social media is all about how your business engages with people. A successful social media campaign will result in people you do not know having positive conversations about your business in the global space of the internet. The difference between social media and many other types of advertising is that it happens on a much larger scale, in real time and potentially out of your control. This has a number of implications:

As a consumer, if I have a good or bad experience with a company I can quickly tell my social media friends and, with a click of a button, they can tell their friends. All of this without the original company being aware (if they are not listening).

As a business, I can develop my social media so that I am engaging with a large number of people. For example, as of May 2011 I have nearly 4,000 Twitter followers, over 300 LinkedIn connections and about 200 Facebook friends. I can have a 'know, like, trust' relationship with far more people that I could possibly interact with on a face to face basis.

All my contacts have chosen to connect with me – they are giving me permission to market to them – though they can easily disconnect if they don't like what I am saying.

The only thing that building this number of relationships has cost me is time. Social media tools are essentially free.

Social media tools

There are a number of tools available to enable this engagement with your audience as shown in the illustration below. These include blogging, newsletters, social networking, internet forums, video and podcasts, articles and press releases. The combination of tools that you choose to use depends upon:

- Your aims for the use of social media

- Your audience

- Your type of business

- Your content

- Your resources

The tools are constantly changing, both in the features available and the techniques for making the best use of them. I'm sure that this time next year, new tools will be available and new ways of using the tools will be suggested. As you decide how you are going to use social media, you should be aware of changes and regularly check that you are still putting your energies into the correct tools, based on the latest developments, changes in your audience, resources and the aims of the business.

Aims

What do you want to get out of social media? Why do you want to use it? Yes, we all ultimately want to get more business, we all want to increase our presence on the internet – but think short term/long term.

For example, initially I wanted to use social media to build my brand, by sharing information which would give me credibility as having knowledge about IT applications. Over time, people have asked me IT related questions on social media and I have received referrals directly through social media tools.

For others, the most important thing is to drive traffic to their website. I am working with a firm that sells pewter miniatures. We need to make sure that people are aware that the website exists and what it sells. We can drive traffic to the website through coordinated use of social media.

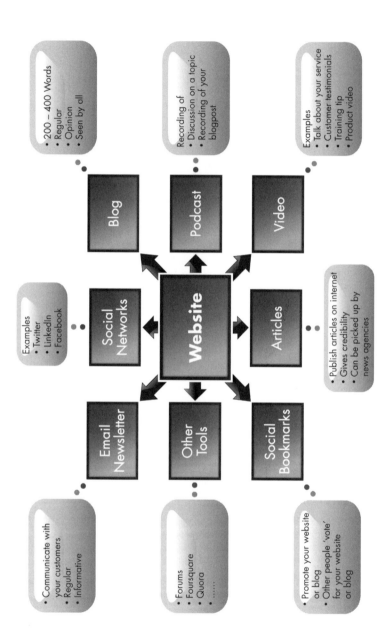

Website

- Blog
  - 200 – 400 Words
  - Regular
  - Opinion
  - Seen by all

- Podcast
  - Recording of
    - Discussion on a topic
    - Recording of your blogpost

- Video
  - Examples
    - Talk about your service
    - Customer testimonials
    - Training tip
    - Product video

- Social Networks
  - Examples
    - Twitter
    - LinkedIn
    - Facebook

- Articles
  - Publish articles on internet
  - Gives credibility
  - Can be picked up by news agencies

- Email Newsletter
  - Communicate with your customers
  - Regular
  - Informative

- Other Tools
  - Forums
  - Foursquare
  - Quora
  - ....

- Social Bookmarks
  - Promote your website or blog
  - Other people 'vote' for your website or blog

For some others, the aim may be to provide customer service, for others it could be unique to them. For example, a sandwich shop could take orders through social media. Depending upon your aims, you may select different tools and use the tools in a unique way. Typical aims could be:

- Brand building

- Drive traffic to website

- Increase footfall in retail shop

- Broadcast news

- Share information

- Provide customer service

- Advertise events and training courses

- Develop awareness about product or service

- Have conversations with people

- Develop engagement

Many of these aims overlap and one may result in the next. Try writing down nine aims on pieces of paper and arrange them in order of importance. You may find that you end up with short term and long term aims.

Success measurements

Consider also how you are going to measure the success of your social media. There are a number of ways you can measure success including:

- Visits to website/blog

- Comments on blog

- Forwarding to others (retweet) of tweets

- Facebook friends or 'likes'

- Twitter followers

- People who view your LinkedIn profile

- Hits on your videos

- Social bookmarking votes

- Podcast downloads

- Recognition at face to face networking based on your online activity

- New business directly through social media

- Referrals through social media

Over time, you need to regularly review your success measures to identify what is working and what needs to be changed. You may need to add more tools, stop using a tool or change the way you use a tool.

Audience

You need to understand who you want to engage with on social media. Your audience will be made up of a number of different groups. Each group may engage with social media in a different way. Consider people in each of the following categories:

Customers	Present, past and future (customers may fall into separate groups; for example, consider both those who use your product or service and those who pay for it).
Suppliers	Your accountant, IT Support and other people you use.
Personal contacts	The people you know through networking or socially.
Staff	Should you use social media for internal staff communication?
Influencers	People that you would like to talk to who could support your services or hold senior positions in your industry. Some may be sources of useful information; some may be in a position to refer your services if you engage with them.
Business partners	Talk to and about business partners on social media – an easy way to promote others
Competitors	Check what your competitors are doing on social media – maybe you don't want to talk to them, but I suggest you listen to them.

Once you have identified contacts in each of these groups, spend some time understanding what social media tools they use. If your audience is mainly on LinkedIn, but not much else, this will indicate that you need to focus your initial efforts on LinkedIn.

For example: many accountancy firms use LinkedIn and Twitter as their primary social media. Last year, I worked with Accountants A. As part of developing their social media strategy, we analysed their potential audience. We discovered that Accountants A had a number of private clients abroad. This indicated that Accountants A should develop a Facebook presence, as this was the tool of choice for those private clients who lived abroad.

Business type

The selection of tools that you decide to use will also be dependent on your business type. A business based entirely in a set location, a shop for example, may want to focus their social media geographically. A business based more nationally, say using a website shop, will be more concerned with national based social media. Some businesses will need to use a combination of approaches.

You should also consider whether you are in a B2B or B2C environment. A different approach to social media may be required.

Content

What are you going to talk about using these tools?

We are a consumer society. On our phone, radio, TV, tablet, etc. we consume information in short sound bursts. How many of you quickly consume the latest news on the internet or keep track of the latest sports scores at a glance?

As a business, you can use the idea of short sound bursts to engage with your audience to market your company. By sharing information and encouraging your audience to give an opinion or comment, you develop a sharing, added value brand around your company.

Think about what information you can share. You may want to give tips or information relevant to your business. You may want to concentrate on being a conduit of knowledge from others.

Social media is meant to be 'Social'. Make sure you don't fall into the trap of always broadcasting or selling. Think about showing a personal side to your social media – how personal is up to you but remember, that unless you are a major brand, people buy from people.

Whatever you say using the social media tools can be seen by everybody and everything you say reflects upon your company brand and values. Consider whether it is appropriate for your 'business' to be talking when in the pub on a Friday night, swearing, or talking about going back to bed as the business is going through a quiet patch. These are all examples that I have seen when listening to businesses on social media.

Each of the tools requires a different style of content – business/personal/ sharing. Make sure you select the tools that are going to be appropriate for the content that you have available or are prepared to share.

Resources

Some companies have decided to spend their marketing budget entirely on digital marketing – putting resources into their website and social media and no longer using traditional print advertising.

At first glance, social media appears to be free – none of the tools discussed need to be paid for. However do not discount the amount of time that it takes to set up your business profiles on these sites and to use the sites on a daily basis. I would always suggest that you start small and use one tool well before adding another tool, rather than taking a scattergun approach and not succeeding with any.

The more time you spend using the social media tools, the more return you will get out of them – but if you are a sole trader, your time will be limited. The time you spend needs to be compared to the time you spend doing other forms of marketing – for example, how long does it take to go to a networking meeting?

As a rough guide, once you have set up your profiles and learnt the associated tools, I would aim to spend approximately the following amount of time on your selected combination. The exact time spent will vary depending upon the focus of your individual strategy.

Tool		Per month (minutes)	Per week (minutes)	Per day (minutes)
Social networks				
	LinkedIn			30
	Twitter			30
	Facebook			20
Blogs			60	
Podcasts		60		
Videos		120		
Articles			60	
Social bookmarks			30	
Other tools			60 (tool dependent)	
Newsletter		180		

Conclusion

Using social media can be a very successful and integral part of your marketing activity and if used appropriately will go some way to building your business growth. The internet is changing and people are talking about businesses whether those businesses are part of the conversation or not. At the very least you ought to be aware of whether people are talking about your business.

Remember:

- Take the time upfront to identify your social media strategy. Think about your aims, your audience, your business type, your content and your resources. Identify the tools that will work for your business.

- Start slowly and build up your activity.

- Don't be a 'lurker', take part in conversations and get to know the people who are interested enough to follow you.

- Don't expect instant results, it takes time to build up a following and develop your contacts. It may take 6 -12 months before you get results. Measure regularly and implement changes appropriately.

Mary Thomas, BSc
Expertise Focus: Social Media

After a Mathematics and Computation degree at Loughborough University, Mary joined Price Waterhouse Management Consultants, initially as a programmer, but quickly moving through design, analysis and project manager. After three years secondment to the US firm and the birth of her son, Mary took a career break for five years.

Not satisfied with not using her brain, during her career break Mary raised over £100,000 to build a new building for the preschool in her local town. Once her children reached school age, Mary looked for a new challenge and joined Oxfordshire Adult Learning as an IT Tutor, achieving her PGCE (FE) in 2006 and her A1 Assessor award in 2008.

After working for a couple of distance learning companies, Mary started Concise Training (http://www.concisetraining.net) in 2008. With an initial emphasis on IT training, helping businesses to use social media became a more substantial part of her business. Using her analysis skills learnt with Price Waterhouse Management Consultants, her underlying IT skills and her knowledge as a trainer, Mary has successfully advised a number of businesses on the best way to make use of this set of powerful tools to engage their audience.

More recently, Mary has worked with City & Guilds to create the first accredited social media qualification at Level 2 and Level 3. Launched in Feb 2011, this assessed qualification develops a good knowledge and understanding of social media as well as the practical knowledge to use the tools. Learners are asked to produce a social media strategy for their business as well as use social media tools in earnest for sixteen weeks. For more information look at http://www.concisetraining.net/social-media-qualification/

Special offer for *Breaking the Barriers to Business Growth* readers: One of the most commonly used social media tools is LinkedIn, readers of *Breaking the Barriers to Business Growth* can access the e-learning Introduction to LinkedIn module produced by Concise Training. Email now for details. trainer@concisetraining.net. Worth £15.

Chapter 8

SEO lost and found

Jonathan Fink

SEO lost and found
Jonathan Fink

Glossary of terms

SEO – Search Engine Optimisation is a methodology for gaining high rankings in search engines under the listings that are 'natural', 'organic', 'algorithmic', or to put it in simple language, 'free'. SEO is the art of increasing enquiries or sales that a website can generate for its owners. Although Google accounts for as much as 70% of search engine queries in the US and UK, there are many search engines that can be targeted with SEO, including blog search, news search, image and video search, social and business media as well as local search and academic search and a range of industry specific vertical search engines, directories and third party aggregators of search results and company listings.

SEM – Search Engine Marketing more typically refers to 'paid advertising' methods of getting more search engine traffic. This can encompass advertising models like Google AdWords, paid placement on third party websites, contextual advertising and other campaign options. SEM is seen as a more holistic approach to gaining sales through various online marketing methods.

SMM – Social Media Marketing is becoming a significant element of integrated marketing communication plans, and blends SEO and SEM to gain higher visibility for your business through the plethora of social and business media sites that have sprung into existence.

PPC – The pay per click model of promoting a website allows advertisers to pay for greater prominence on a search engine or website. For search engines like Google, the display of the advert is triggered by keyword phrases typed into the search box, though the advertiser is only charged if a user clicks on their advert, and that click is deemed to be valid and non fraudulent.

CMS – Content Management Systems allow many people to contribute to and manage websites and other repositories of content in a 'collaborative environment'. These systems can be located 'in the cloud' and accessed online to allow users to change their website remotely, or they may be installed as software on a server or on individual PCs. Without a CMS, websites are typically stored as a series of 'flat files', but this makes SEO, editing and publishing difficult.

Start your search for more information at:

http://en.wikipedia.org/wiki/Seo

http://en.wikipedia.org/wiki/Search_engine_marketing

http://en.wikipedia.org/wiki/Social_Media_Marketing

http://en.wikipedia.org/wiki/Pay_per_click

http://en.wikipedia.org/wiki/Content_Management_System

Introduction

If poorly planned, SEO is doomed to fail – and leave sales opportunities untapped. Without exception, websites that dominate their industry sectors have a logical strategy and marketing plan that underlie their site structure and online campaigns. Part of this structure is a clear articulation of what they do, for whom, when and why. SEO is not about finding words that are frequently searched on and splurging them all over your site. It involves understanding what your customers buy and when, what the problem is that they are trying to solve and using SEO to articulate your offering in a way that ensures you are highly ranked in search engines on the highly specific and 'targeted' language that your prospects use.

This chapter is built on assumptions that may not be shared by all marketing experts, but can be succinctly expressed as a series of 'informed opinions'. Experience has convinced this author that only a planned and engineered approach to SEO can bring success. SEO is neither arcane, nor a 'dark art', but is all too often implemented in a simplistic, unimaginative, lazy and misguided way. SEO can fail to fulfil the aspirations of a business owner in numerous ways, and there are considerable risks involved in paying an external agency for SEO or PPC services. But the reward of successful SEO is the creation of a predictable and sustainable source of new sales that can contribute strongly to the growth of your business. SEO is often the lowest cost method for acquiring new customers there is. SEO is only one channel out of many marketing methods you will need to perfect to sustain the growth of your business, but can become the natural 'hub' for all your online and offline marketing campaigns and activities.

Connections and results

The web inspires some dizzying numbers with billions of web pages materialising in only a few years and daily searches rising from nothing to hundreds of millions per day. The opportunity can seem boundless, the potential profit infinite. But everything has limits, and any business owner with a website comes up against these limits almost straight away. They build a site but no one comes – at least too few visitors to sustain a real world business model. They try pay-per-click advertising, but the cost of attracting new customers exceeds any reasonable margin they might make on sale of their products or services. With 'boundless' online opportunities also come seemingly limitless competitors and barriers to growth.

What's it for? – SEO only exists to gain results. A result is typically a qualified enquiry or sale. If your leads or sales do not go up substantially in the first six months of deploying SEO, then it's not working. If you're not sure if SEO is delivering results, then chances are its failed and you need to rethink your strategy or supplier of SEO services, quickly.

What it's not – SEO is not a magic bullet or a panacea to a business' problems. SEO can't fix a broken business model, and won't dramatically improve the margins on your sales. SEO can't conjure up markets that don't exist or new customers where there is no demand. But where you have a genuine offering in a strong market SEO can help your business grow and prosper.

Your audience

The problem with many practitioners of SEO is that they have a technical rather than a sales and marketing background. Along with their clients they fail to identify in detail who they are tying to sell to, what the full features and characteristics of their product or service are, what's unique about them as a supplier. They fail to articulate any key benefits and outline the problems they solve. In a word, they fail to address their audience, and when a website lacks the keywords and content that express all of the above, it damages its potential to rank in search engines at all, or attract new prospects to its offering.

Commerce first – search engines exist to connect people to information.

Relevance is the key to their success, and the key to getting better results for your business online. Any SEO strategy that places the perceived needs of a search engine ahead of its customers is doomed. SEO can't be obviously artificial and robotic in character or it runs the risk of being penalised.

Searches second – The 'algorithmic' demands of search engines are a secondary consideration. Your site must be compelling for clients primarily, and if SEO has grown your web traffic, but not increased your lead pipeline, then it's failing to excite your audience. There is a chance your messages and keywords are not 'targeted' enough for the audience you are selling to.

Things in the right order

When business owners think of increasing web sales, their natural impulse is to 'redesign' first. But when you completely revamp your website it's easy to lose sight of the reasons why you are doing that. The need to focus on design, logos and branding can be a distraction from the real goal – selling. Content, sales processes, optimisation and calls-to-action tend to become an afterthought in the project, and are either left out or weakened. For SEO to work, your entire strategy and website structure need to be geared around the aim of gaining high rankings and providing a compelling and clear sales message.

Planning from principles – you need a plan not only for the 'go-live' version of your site, but a scheme that recognises in 6, 9 or 12 months time the aspirations of your business may have changed. You need to be able to add new client testimonials, new products and news to your site for SEO and for users' benefits. Without a plan, your site may stagnate rather than evolve.

Design, technology, marketing – following the principle that sales come first, the correct order for a web project is: implement web analytics, improve sales processes and conversion rates, perfect your content and site structure, implement lead generating campaigns, get control of your site's content, and then redesign. Plan marketing first, then technology and design last!

Engines and more

Marketing on the web has always been about more than just attaining high search engine rankings. Now that's truer than ever, with a plethora of online 'channels' that can help you generate leads and sales. From social and business media sites to directories, industry press, news portals, forums and blogs, you should look at your website as merely one 'node' in a network of content that spans the web. If your marketing strategy does not include the regular development and distribution of content around the web, then it is missing out on one of the most powerful and rewarding aspects of web marketing.

Google and the rest – from video to white papers, news content to forum postings the opportunities to get your message across are numerous. But a good SEO strategy will look at what your best ranked competitors are doing and seek to emulate it. Collectively they will have poured hundreds of hours of work into their link building strategies, so 'steal' from the best!

Beyond search engines – social media (i.e. Facebook) tends to be more relevant to B2C offerings and business media sites (i.e. LinkedIn) more beneficial to B2B suppliers. But the same principles that apply to off-line networking also apply online – find out if your prospects actually use a particular website before you pour hundreds of hours into marketing through it.

Arcane arts

SEO is 'Frankenstein' marketing – a hideous blend of science and art, which is repulsive to many traditional marketers, bewildering for business owners and apparently 'easy' to those technical practitioners who often get the subject so wrong. Ironically, it is the technically adept who are most confident in applying SEO, but least qualified to practise it. For some larger corporate sites, fiddling with web files, tuning code and optimising servers may yield impressive results. But for smaller businesses, the 'technical' approach to SEO can be expensive and is largely fruitless. Smaller websites need to work much harder to achieve exceptional results, and their content should focus on their online customers.

Content and messaging – focus on your content, messages and ways in which you can compel customers to express an interest in your offering. It helps to articulate in keywords things like quality of service (unique, individual, professional), pricing criteria (exclusive, cost-effective, discount, cheap) and even who you are (agency, company, vendor, expert, specialist).

Links and relationships – apart from content and keywords, links are the other major influence that determines why sites rank highly in search engines. But instead of creating hundreds of links from sites that have little connection and relevance to your business, focus on building a smaller number of strong strategic relationships with other websites, expressed as 'links'.

Grow a tail

The 'long tail' is a statistical concept popularized by Chris Anderson in a Wired magazine article of 2004, and further elaborated on in his book *The Long Tail: Why the Future of Business Is Selling Less of More* (ISBN 1-4013-0237-8). In the last few years 'Long Tail' has been used to describe the online retailing strategy of selling a vast range of products in relatively small volumes, exemplified by websites such as iTunes, Amazon and Netflix. This 'virtual' approach to the supply of goods overturns traditional models of business that are held back by the cost and physical limits of storing inventory. But the 'long tail' can also be beneficial when considering keyword optimisation for high search engine rankings. The principle suggests that rather than focusing SEO only on a handful of highly competitive phrases that deliver large volumes of visitors to your site, you also optimise for thousands of longer, targeted phrases.

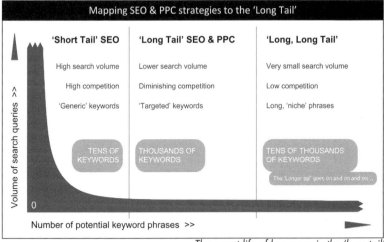

The secret life of language in the 'long tail'

The secret life of language – In any given industry there will be tens of phrases at the head of the tail. These 'short tail' phrases will be associated with high search volumes, but competition will be fierce to get in a crucial top 10 positions on Google's search pages. Where phrases become more 'targeted', small business websites have a better chance of ranking highly and can also deploy them in PPC campaigns. Competition may remain high, but so also may the monthly volume of searches being done on given phrases. The real opportunity and challenge is to tap into the 'long, long tail', where search volumes drop to as few as 2-3 a year, but the number of potential 'phrase permutations' can grow into the hundreds of thousands.

Engineered deployment of SEO – Where a website can deploy great diversity of content, it may also experience better conversion rates, as users finding the site come to a page exactly in line with their search query. In the 'long, long tail', language has a secret life that few businesses are aware of – but which can be unlocked by asking questions such as: 'what are we selling, and to whom', 'what are the characteristics of our products', 'when do they buy and why; is it on quality, price, features or service.' All these questions can be expressed with keywords, and each phrase can attract potential clients – but it takes a planned, 'engineered' approach to optimisation to effectively deploy 1,000s of keywords across a business website.

Start your search for more information at: http://en.wikipedia.org/wiki/Long_Tail

Read more about 'long tail' economics: http://www.amazon.co.uk/Longer-Long-Tail-Creating-Unlimited/dp/1847940366

Will they come if you build it?

'Build it and they'll come' was one of the first clichés and fallacies of online marketing. Most websites fail to fulfil their owners' commercial objectives, simply because they can't be found. Many other sites, once found, fail to compel their audience to take any action, let alone make a purchase. Even if a website is perceived to be working by its owners, they often don't have the stats in place to understand which bit of their online marketing is working and which isn't. That lack of insight makes it impossible to make informed decisions about where to scale up marketing activities and which campaigns to push. But every visitor comes from somewhere, and every journey which ends in a purchase has a beginning that can be tracked and traced back to source. To invest more in what works and dump what doesn't (fast!), requires a business owner to be really engaged with their website, and have complete control over it.

What is a result? – The first step is to define what a result is. This sounds absurd, but every site that has not articulated its offering well, also probably has little concept of what it wants to achieve online beyond 'a nice looking site'. You must be able to measure success, or it won't be clear where to invest time, effort and money or how to evolve and scale your site in future.

Measure, measure, measure – A gradation of results is advisable, to measure every aspect of user behaviour. From 'positive interactions' such as viewing a video or downloading a white paper, to completion of a newsletter sign-up, your goals will tell you important things about how customers are reacting to your messages, site and offering. Of course completed enquiry forms, or purchases are the real goal of SEO, but you must ensure you can trace these back to the keywords or campaigns that prompted the visit to find your site to build on that success.

Rewards don't come without risk and SEO can be a very chancy business. When they enter the online arena, site owners often forget the sound business instincts they exercise in the off-line world. But the same rules apply: when working with an SEO consultant or full-service marketing agency constantly ask if the relationship is working. Before commissioning a project check out their credentials and successes; have they worked for a company in your sector and can they provide references? Don't rely on just one source for your leads such as SEO or PPC, but build multiple channels to market, and seek to perfect each of them into a cost-effective channel. And the simple rule when practicing SEO is to remember, if you can't tell if it's working – then it's not. If enquiries are not growing, or the quality is poor then your SEO is misguided and you should rethink or experiment some more. If you are not sure what your SEO agency is doing for you, and they can't explain, then chances are they are doing nothing at all. Change your supplier, take control of SEO and take ownership of its successes and mistakes; become an expert.

Read more about this subject: http://www.seochat.com/

Work with an SEO expert to generated more sales:
http://www.momentumws.co.uk/

Jonathan Fink
Expertise: Search Engine Optimisation (SEO) and Digital Marketing for sales growth

Jonathan Fink is Managing Director of Momentum Web Solutions and a partner in Right Angle Consultants (RAC).

Momentum is a strategic web marketing company, founded in 2005, that has gained experience working with high growth companies from ambitious small businesses through to large corporate organisations. Momentum exists to help its clients generate more sales through their online activities. It achieves this through the use of a unique methodology and cutting edge technologies, supported by training and consultancy that is amongst the most advanced in the industry. Momentum has a team of imaginative marketing, copywriting and coding experts to support its work.

Although fanatical about SEO and with many years hands-on experience, Jonathan still needs to justify the 'art' that he practises on clients' web sites almost daily. Because he operates in an industry that for the most part is unregulated, has no generally accepted standards, is constantly changing, and is poorly understood, he believes that being open about what SEO is and what it can realistically achieve is paramount. Many business have been 'stung' by ignorant, chaotic and unscrupulous SEO consultants and agencies and Jonathan works hard to ensure his client are not disappointed with the result his work brings. His SEO is totally sales and results driven.

Jonathan is unusual in the SEO industry because his background is in linguistics and languages and his passion revolves around words. Through Momentum he has fused these interests and combined them with his previous work experience as a strategic management consultant, to create an absolutely unique and effective approach to online marketing.

Special offer for *Breaking the Barriers to Business Growth* **readers:** A FREE 'Competitor Spotlight' report to show which websites dominate your industry online and why. Take the first step to becomes a leader in your sector online and request this analysis and FREE half hour phone consulting session worth £175: www.momentumws.co.uk/spotlight

Chapter 9

Planning for growth: how to stop your IT hitting the fan

Mark Salisbury

Planning for growth: how to stop your IT hitting the fan
Mark Salisbury

Introduction

Over the years, we have seen many different attitudes to running the IT side of small and growing businesses, and been able to formulate some ideas of what to do and what not to do to ensure your businesses can succeed and grow.

Start with the future in mind

The most important aspect is a strategic one. What do you want your business to look like in, say, three or five years from now? How big will it be, how fast will you grow, how many staff will you have, what will your offices be like, if any, what will your operations be, and who will your customers be? The answers to these questions should inform the whole business growth strategy, and the IT side no less than any other aspect.

Enabler or necessary evil?

Then you need to firmly decide your attitude to IT. In a very few cases you can safely decide that IT is peripheral to your business, and you might be able to get away with minimal thought and expense. In the overwhelming majority of businesses, though, IT will be the enabler of your business. It is the tool that all your staff use every day. It will make your staff more efficient, or let you work remotely, or let you open other branches, or it might be what makes your business even possible. In these cases, then, you need to recognise that IT is a core essential, and you need to treat it appropriately.

When making strategic or technical decisions, then, you will need to bear the IT aspect in mind, in the same way you might consider the human resources, finance or workflow. The most successful organisations have someone responsible for IT on the board or in senior management at least. This allows IT considerations and possibilities to contribute to your business plans for maximum advantage.

The IT role

If you are to have someone in your team who is going to be responsible for IT

- it must be a formal part of their job, and
- they must have the expertise to do it properly.

Would you trust your financial planning or preparation of your company accounts or servicing your car to someone who isn't knowledgeable in the area? Neither should you expect 'the person who knows most about computers' to be a good enough IT champion or resource. Besides, as you grow, the IT role will grow together with the expertise required.

The role is not just business-as-usual – supporting staff and dealing with problems; it's improving the way your business uses information, better processes, improved resources and resilience, new ways of working, remaining competitive.

If your business doesn't warrant having IT true expertise in a strategic role, or in an operational role, it is a small-minded mistake to try to tack it onto someone's job role. IT strategy, IT implementation and IT support is something you should outsource if you are not prepared to do it properly in-house.

Why outsource?

There is a catalogue of reasons why outsourcing makes sense for IT. I believe that the key ones for growth are these:

As you grow, your IT needs to adapt with your organisation. Typically an internal person won't have gained the experience of working in an organisation that's like the one you are to become. Typically outsourcers have experience of a range of businesses.

You will occasionally need niche IT skills; it makes no sense paying the premium for rarely used skills to be in-house.

Outsourcing is a way to get the specific skills, experience and expertise you need, and only pay for what you need, when you need it.

IT Strategy, Project work and Desktop Support are very different. All are important. Are you prepared to spread your resources thinly so that an internal person can do it all themselves?

Running IT systems, servers and projects isn't your business's core activity. You should focus on what you do best, what you deliver to your customers. Make that as efficient, automated, and profitable as possible, and let an IT expert run your IT with the same approach.

You probably don't have the staff development and career progression that the kind of IT people you need are looking for. That means that if you do hire them, you will lose them when they want to move up.

An internal staff member who has responsibility for IT support only as part of their job is going to be interrupted in their work to the point of insanity.

IT support is improved by the economies of scale. An outsourcer has the scale that you are unlikely to reach.

Staff & efficiency

Too many organisations hire staff without regard to how well they are going to be able to use the main business tool provided for them, namely their computer and its software.

Computer skills should play a part in your recruitment decisions. Once hired, you should ensure that your new employees and their tools are working at peak efficiency by providing training. Your benchmark should be that computer users know all the capabilities and features of the software at their disposal, or else they will be always in second gear meaning you are wasting money and time, and keeping your productivity and growth limited.

At the same time you should ensure that you are providing the right software to your team. There might be a much better way for them to do their jobs with a different piece of software. For example, consider using a database instead of a collection of spreadsheets. Find a way for your staff to share contacts and information, maybe a CRM system or a master contact list everyone can update. Has a program been published which is specific to your industry that might improve your workflow or process?

You'll already know that you should have documented processes which are followed to perform your organisation's workflow. To make sure your staff are as efficient as possible, find out what parts of their jobs are repetitive, time-consuming and mindless. See if you can automate those parts (even very small parts), so your staff can spend their mental energies on tasks better suited to humans. A 'macro' is a simple computer program that can perform a predictable/set sequence of actions such as keystrokes and mouse clicks. You are most likely to have experienced macros in Microsoft Excel where recording your own macro is an easy toolbar option. But macros can be used to automate almost any pre-set/predictable actions on a computer, including opening an application or file, waiting for a popup box to appear before clicking the correct button, sending an email. You don't need to have programming skills to make some macros either, though it helps a lot. Very affordable software exists which will write macros for you.

If you create lots of contracts, letters, proposals etc., consider document automation software which will create new documents from a template, filling in all the fields properly thus saving hours and ensuring a document isn't sent with someone else's data in it.

You should also be keen on 'single data entry', which means that the organisation enters a piece of information (e.g. a customer's phone number or address) once and once only, and it's shared/copied between the applications and people that need it. If you need to change it, do so in one place, and have the change propagated.

Policies

You should also have policies in place for computer use covering aspects such as passwords, email and internet usage, personal use of company computing resources and data security. It should also cover how/whether to send multi-recipient or bulk emails.

The majority of security breaches are attributable to staff behaviour, most of it not malevolent. You should definitely have a password or passphrase complexity policy, but be careful not to make the burden too onerous or else you will end up with ridiculously predictable passwords or post-it notes on desks. Users can be tricked into defeating even the most fortified network, for example by clicking on malicious pop-ups or giving away their passwords. Staff education ought to be the cornerstone of your security policy.

Grant privileges to users only as necessary, limiting access to sensitive data.

Any sensitive data that does or might leave your organisation should be encrypted. Consider having all laptops and removable media such as DVDs or USB storage, secured in this way. The same considerations apply to smartphones. Assume they are going to be lost or stolen, and that they'll be accessed by others. Will your business thrive in this situation? Will there be advantage to the competition? Will you suffer reputational damage?

Backup and disaster recovery

Backup is securing copies of files in case they are lost or damaged.

You should:

- make backups often enough so that if you have lost the originals you don't have too much work to repeat to get back to where you were (the frequency of backup depends on this: it might be weekly, daily, or even every few minutes for certain files or databases);

- regularly test backups to make sure they run properly and that you really can recover files from them;

- encrypt your backup media (stealing backup tapes might be easier than hacking your server);

- store your backup media somewhere they won't suffer from fire or theft that affects an entire site; and

- consider secure online backup if your connection is fast enough.

You should also have a Disaster Recovery ('DR') plan, and IT should be an aspect of it. Consider the various realistic possibilities. Include the possibility of a malware outbreak, power cuts and loss of internet access, loss of servers and destruction of a site as scenarios. Work out what you would do. How, where and for how long could you operate like that? How would you regain full operation? What is the maximum time that you could manage without this or that facility or computer system? There are often plenty of things that can be done to mitigate the downtime and improve the resilience of IT systems.

Business computer ranges

Computer hardware technology is improving all the time. This is great news if your computing use needs a great deal of processing power or seems to be taking too long. However, because new PC models are available every week, maintaining any consistency in what computer hardware you use (to gain efficiency and financial benefits from sticking to one model) would seem unattainable.

Don't buy whatever seems to give you the best deal on the day. Making the right choice matters.

Leading computer manufacturers (such as HP and DELL) have certain business ranges of PC, notebook and server which stay fairly consistent from one month, or year to the next, and these are what you should be buying. This means that spare parts for repairs are available for an extended period, and that you can replace a machine with another bought at a different time with relatively little hassle. This will save you money in the medium to long term, as well as minimising business disruption.

Financing

Purchasing computers can be a significant capital outlay. You might see significant cashflow advantages in leasing your computers instead of outright purchase. You might be able to get a leasing deal and you are normally able to finance the whole purchase including the software costs, any setup labour, warranty and even ongoing support for the computer. I am told that leasing could be better than purchase for tax reasons too. This strategy will enable you to leverage your finances better and grow your computer counts faster than having to spend your cash.

Software licensing

Usually when you buy a PC you have the option of bundling the operating system and office productivity software at reduced cost. Avoid this as there are significant advantages in holding and managing your software licenses and media centrally. For example if you use Microsoft Office, wouldn't you prefer your whole team to be using the same version so they can all share documents? To get onto the volume license schemes a minimum purchase of 5 (at once) is required, and no consideration is given for copies you have already bought piecemeal. You can also decide to buy 'software assurance' which means all those licensed machines will be entitled to the latest versions whenever they are released. If you can afford the cash, buy your 5 'volume' licenses in one go, using them for your next 5 machines as you buy them (cheaper overall), and thereafter you will be able to add licenses in smaller increments. Better still, get a good price for buying the next five machines now and having them made ready for use: you'll have spares until they are deployed to specific users.

On site warranty

However you acquire your computer hardware, you would be advised to spend a fraction more and enhance the warranty. Think about whether you are happy to send the PC or server back to the manufacturer for repair, or would you rather one of their technicians came to you, same day or next day. If you have spare machines, this will affect your recovery timetable.

Infrastructure

As your organisation grows, your team members will increasingly need to share facilities and services, such as email, calendars, files, backup and printing. You will want to facilitate central management of your computers in such areas as security and anti virus deployment. This is what servers are for. In time you may need multiple servers for different purposes. The options are rapidly changing:

Virtual Machines: You can simultaneously run multiple servers 'virtual machines' on the very same (beefy) physical hardware giving enormous capital, space and running efficiency advantages. Your IT people will find it easier to test software as they can easily make a copy of a real server for testing; resilience will be enhanced and disaster recovery will be facilitated.

Some of the IT services you need such as email & collaboration, backup, antivirus, accounting packages, even 'office' applications can already be purchased from specialist providers on 'the cloud' who do all the technical work such as providing and maintaining the servers & software and making sure the data is backed up. This might save you both capital and running costs as you might not need that extra server, the IT maintenance costs or a beefier PC, just a better internet connection. And you'll pay based on your usage, which is great as your size changes. Over time the range and complexity of what is available via the net will only increase.

Your IT is the tool your staff use to run your business every day. Plan and resource it properly to ensure you get the best performance and efficiency.

Mark Salisbury BSc, ARCS, MIoD
Expertise Focus: IT

Mark is a Director of The Oxford Knowledge
Company, a group of articulate, educated, business-
friendly IT experts.

Many businesses do not have the staff to take care
of their own IT needs. The Oxford Knowledge
Company fills the gaps.

For some organisations this means serving as the
partly- or fully-outsourced IT department: providing
advice; installing computer systems; performing regular preventative
maintenance – all to ensure the smooth running of their businesses. For others
it means complementing the in-house team by providing expertise, experience
or systems: in a strategic consultancy role; to fill skills gaps; to provide extra
resources as required; offering holiday or sickness cover.

For all clients it means understanding their long term business objectives and
designing technology solutions that will enable them to reach these goals
as their businesses grow. The real key is getting involved strategically and
allowing the clients to focus on what they do best.

In previous lives, Mark was a physicist at Imperial College, London and later
at the Joint European Torus nuclear fusion project. He has also spent 4 years
as a Broadcast Systems Engineer at BBC television.An ex-Argentine Tango
teacher, he is a keen dancer, particularly LindyHop and Salsa. He also enjoys
yachting.

Special offer for *Breaking the Barriers to Business Growth* **readers:**
As IT is an area steeped in expertise and jargon, you might not know where to
start, or what kind of shape your organisation is in.

As you have already demonstrated that you are determined to plan
for growth by reading this book, I invite you to visit http://okco.net/
BreakingBarriersOffer to find an exclusive offer for a free IT review. The no-
obligation report we'll provide will help you identify the risks your business is
exposed to, and identify cost-effective ways to improve computer network and
employee productivity.

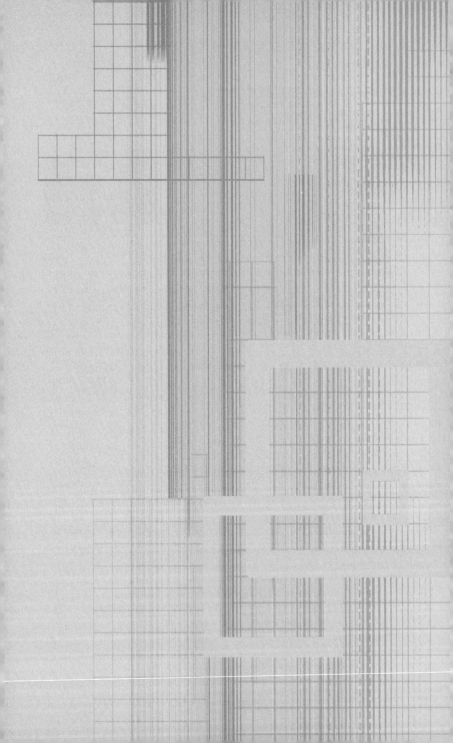

Chapter 10

Leadership presence:
how to get buy in

Sarah McCloughry

Leadership presence: how to get buy in
Sarah McCloughry

"Your ability to negotiate, communicate, influence, and persuade others to do things is absolutely indispensable to everything you accomplish in life." Brian Tracy, business leader, author and multi-millionaire

As a leader of a fast growing business at a time of maximum risk and maximum opportunity, you are influencing everyone who comes into your orbit. You will have been technically extremely competent when the company was small and perfectly formed. Now however, you are likely to feel under pressure to keep ahead of the game. You have a vision for your company and have to take the lead so others follow – you've had to win trust, agreement and investment. Things are changing – you have to become a different kind of leader.

You are inspiring people with your vision as well as your product. You need to persuade others to believe in you, to follow you, to accept your ideas, your arguments and especially your point of view so you win their agreement. Because what they are buying into is your vision.

And the decision makers that you have to keep on side who enhance or fatally undermine your company are many. Amongst them are:

- Your customers
- Your suppliers
- Your staff
- Your board and chairman
- Your investors
- Your bank
- The key influencers in your network
- And, especially, your spouse or partner

You are the leader. How do you get people to follow you and buy your vision? How do you build trust and belief so others are as persuaded as you are? How do you inspire confidence, come across as credible, arouse respect, win trust and ultimately, achieve the buy in for your vision?

That first agreement you make, the one that you have put most effort and thought into is built on trust. The decision maker, whether your customer, your staff or your partner doesn't know yet whether your vision and indeed your solution really does what you say it does. Only when they have bought for a second time do they know that you were right – or not! The first buy in is based on the relationship you have forged, the trust you have earned. It's based on their belief in you. The decision maker buys a first time because they believe you and buy next time because they believe in what you are selling.

You might be astonished to learn how quickly we make decisions

Every decision that gets made takes place 7 seconds before in the unconscious. Conscious thinking only kicks in afterwards to modify or alter that initial decision.

The decision made in the unconscious tends to be far more accurate than any decision based on conscious thinking.

To get the other person to agree to commit their time, energy and/or money with you, they rely on what they know of you and your track record, what they know of the product or service, what you say and what you do. You influence the decision maker by impacting their unconscious process. To do this, it's about who you are.

As a leader, your role is to get people to follow you. As I said, your first agreement will be because you are trusted – you convince people to believe you, believe what you say is true, they place their confidence in your judgement. How did you do that?

Leadership presence is that added magic unconscious influencer that creates the conditions for buy in. It's in your intention, your attitude, your behaviour, your performance – who and how you are with your audience. In creating 'presence', 3 things are happening at the same time. These unconscious influencers are:

- What's going on inside you (your "inner game", your intention)

- What's going on outwardly (your external process, how you manage your unconscious communication and your language)

- What's going on with your audience (how you read your impact and respond to signals).

The "Inner Game"
What's going on in your head?

What's going on inside you is fundamental to your ability to influence others. It is determined by how convinced you are, how well you influence yourself. And there is no point in pretending – people will sniff out a mismatch between what's in your head and what you are doing. You cannot put on a mask and expect to get away with it

The watcher's unconscious mind will perceive and log your facial expressions and body language even if they don't consciously notice them. So you will be spotted, whether you like it or not.

People are likely to be unconsciously picking up from you to determine their decision to trust you and hence buy in. They will be asking themselves:

- Do you believe in yourself – can they trust your judgement if you don't trust in your own? How well do you influence yourself positively?

- Your self awareness – do you have inner knowledge of your strengths and how to play them?

- Are you optimistic – do you believe in future possibilities and opportunities?

- Your motivation – how hungry are you? How badly do you want this? By how much?

- Your integrity – can they rely on you, your truthfulness and your honesty?

- wYour intention – are you clear as to your mission for yourself and your team?

- Your purposefulness – are you are certain and sure of your direction?

- Your drive – are you excited and inspired by your vision? Are you willing to commit the energy to make it a reality?

- Your determination – are you resilient and steady in 'holding the line' under fire? Are you unshakable in the face of adversity?

- Your commitment – are you prepared to sacrifice, give up and give away a great deal to stay loyal to your promise? Do you mean it?

- Your self discipline – are you ready to strive all day and every day to fulfill your objectives? Are you rigorous about planning and preparation? Do you prioritise your time and attention?

- Self care – do you exercise and pay attention to your own health and other needs? Do you give yourself time away from the office? Do you spend time with friends and family?

- Your gravitas – do you take what you do and what you believe (though not yourself) seriously?

Your outward face

These are the unconscious influencers you broadcast to others. Often these go unnoticed though leave a lasting impression.

Your presentation – your audience will be assessing how you dress, how you take care of your appearance, how you hold yourself, your poise, your manner.

Your focus – how you concentrate on the task in hand whilst taking the other person into consideration. They are well aware of the quality and depth of your listening.

Your communication – your body language demonstrates your attention, appropriate register of language, your voice, your delivery, tone, pitch and your listening style. All these are relaxed, pleasing and persuasive.

Your impact

As important as who you are and how you come across is what's going on for your audience. You have to get them on-side in order to lead their thinking and decision making.

- PLU – you have 'People Like Us' skills that mean others quickly identify with you and your best interests.

- Audience know-how – you read your decision maker accurately so you know what they are thinking. You listen intelligently. You are persuasive, encouraging and decisive. You make the decision maker feel good about themselves in your company. They respond positively in the short, medium and long term because you have demonstrated their value to you as a person, not just what you can get from them.

- Events – you constantly anticipate events and stage-manage them to your advantage.

To be a leader, you have already worked out your objectives and vision for your company. When you come into a room, you immediately convey purpose because you're clear as to why you are there and what outcome you seek. You will have already written a business plan – what about a plan for your own life? Look very closely at your personal goals and how they marry with the vision for your company. You aren't likely to be tied to the company you are with forever. Indeed, you will have an exit plan of some sort, even if it takes the next 10 – 20 years. To be clear about where you are headed and what you want to accomplish during that time and afterwards be sure about what you want right now.

There is a finger-like part of the brain called the Reticular Cortex. It helps you to create a magnetic vision – whenever you think of red sports cars, then you keep encountering them. When you are clear as to what it is you want and how this person or these people will help you, it opens you to opportunities to fulfil your vision, it gives you a sense of urgency and energy that makes you far more magnetic – and attractive. And it attracts you to the right people who respond in the way you want them to.

What is your intention? This addresses a much bigger issue of what your values are, what's important to you. You will know whether what you are doing is taking you towards what you value or away from it. It means being in the right place at the right time engaged in the right activity. This points back to how important it is for you to have evolved a personal vision for yourself aligned with who you are. You know exactly what you intend in being with this person and why. You know your direction and purpose – it reinforces your "presence" in the room.

Having leadership presence means that your attention is fully present. Inspiring leaders give their absolute attention to the matter in hand which makes them extremely attractive. People turn round when they enter a room, not because they make a big noise, but because they bring their whole concentration and focus into the present moment.

When President Bill Clinton visited Oxford, a friend of mine noted his charisma as he came into the room. "When he looked at me, it was as though I was the only person in the room that mattered to him." He found this quality extraordinarily magnetic. When you give your fullest attention to what you are doing, you create a powerful bow wave of energy that impacts the decision maker – it was so powerful in Bill Clinton's case that America voted him president twice.

Because you win people's attention immediately with your leadership presence, you command further attention by your movement, your gestures and especially in your speaking. You have condensed and concentrated your power and energy to a fine point in this present moment. This gives you gravitas and presence. You don't dance attention on others, they are keen to please you.

When you are fully present, you speak sparingly and to the point – you have transparent clarity. You communicate easily and precisely so your meaning is absolutely clear. There is no barrier between what comes out of your mouth and what is understood in the other person's brain. When you have listened to people intelligently, read them accurately and positioned yourself as someone who understands and cares for their best interests, this is powerfully attractive.

Having leadership presence inspires others to follow you, be guided by you, say "yes" to you. They respect and support your interests. They're willing to take risks for you; they engineer opportunities for you. They do all this because they have hope in and expectations of you. They believe in you. You are their leader.

Sarah McCloughry
Expertise Focus: Personal Branding

Sarah McCloughry is founder and director of Anrah Training & Development, which help business owners and their senior team cultivate influence. Clients include the Committee on Climate Change, Barclays Commercial, Oxford University, sportscotland, Who's Who and Astrium (EADS).

Sarah is a consultant, trainer and author with a background in theatre, education, psychology, hypnotherapy and coaching. She ran a highly successful Oxford hypnotherapy clinic for 26 years working with business people to promote their 'inner game' to win others over with championship level self-confidence. She has given expert advice in several publications such as 'She' magazine, 'Bella' and 'Zest' and has appeared on national TV, including Channel 5.

For more details about Sarah's service and products, please visit: www.anrah.co.uk

Special offer for *Breaking The Barriers To Business Growth* readers:

In this chapter "Leadership Presence: How To Get Buy In" I introduce you to three strategies to win agreement and business through the power of your personality.

If you'd like to know more about how to gain an edge read my White Paper "How To Cultivate Gravitas" http://wp.me/PBNj6-3Q or email me at sarah@anrah.co.uk and I'll be happy to send you this free report.

Chapter 11

The principle of pre-eminence: 3 KEY strategies to ensure you stand out and become the expert in your business sector

Andrew Ludlam

The principle of pre-eminence: 3 KEY strategies to ensure you stand out and become the expert in your business sector

Andrew Ludlam

Imagine being known as the expert in your industry, being regarded as the authority. It's something that every business owner should aspire to, and more importantly, work towards becoming. In this chapter I shall explore, as well as reveal, some of the specific strategies that you must implement to become the 'go to' resource within your market.

Know thy client

In exploring how best to develop a strategy for positioning your company as an authority, we should start with the most important and critical element in your business: the client.

You need to truly appreciate and understand your clients: who they are, where they are and essentially why they should want to buy from you. See your business from their side of the fence.

Today more than ever before, we have so many marketing messages competing for our attention, and therefore so many more options and choices regarding the products and services we might like to use. Or to put it more succinctly: your prospect has so many more options. If the marketing message you use doesn't talk directly to your audience, doesn't address, or recognise their problem in a compelling and persuasive manner, they will simply go elsewhere.

I often refer to this as the 'Missing Link', simply because I see so many businesses put out marketing materials that essentially fail to speak and connect directly with their audience. There is often something missing: a true understanding of the market place and what it wants.

So how does this notion relate itself to positioning you or your company as an authority in your field? It's fundamental to how you conduct yourself, and how you connect with your market. Experts 'get' their clients, and at a very deep level: they truly know and understand their market.

Have you ever been talking with someone who clearly was an authority, who really knew their topic? How did he or she come across? I imagine there was an air of 'relaxed certainty'; he or she was both knowledgeable and assured. This is exactly what you need to convey, both one-to-one with the client and throughout your marketing materials.

Permeate all of your marketing with a sense of truly understanding and knowing your client's concerns, challenges and anxieties.

Be very honest: if I were to visit your website today, or read your emails, or look at your marketing literature; is it obvious that you know your sector? In other words, do you offer an education to your audience, and not just a sales message? Remember 'experts' don't need to sell, at least not initially. Start to get into the habit of offering your market something of stand-alone value. Educate first, sell second.

Understand that a client never actually buys a product or service: they are buying the result of that product or service. So when crafting your marketing materials talk in terms of 'outcomes': what the client will be left with, after they have engaged your services or used your product. Your prospective client has no real interest in what you do, only in what you can do for them.

Notice how these very simple strategies will start to help you be regarded as the preferred choice. It's by no means all of the answer, but it's a very good starting point and something your competitors will simply not be doing. Whilst they simply talk about themselves, and how great they are, you on the other hand, will demonstrate and purposely articulate a deep understanding and appreciation for your client – which ultimately is all that matters.

The client experience is everything

Whenever I initially ask a business owner as to what makes their company unique, special, or different, a very common response is "We provide excellent customer service". Many companies promise 'excellent customer service' and will position their uniqueness by this notion, however, how many actually deliver on this promise, or more importantly over-deliver?

Excellent customer service these days is a given – we all expect it. It's simply not enough to differentiate yourself from the rest of the crowd. 'Customer service' needs to be something much more effective, demonstrable and above all tangible.

It's even more important if you operate in a heavily commoditized market. You play a dangerous game if you keep trying to offer a 'cheaper widget', especially as margins become tighter and tighter. However, you can always out-play the competition by providing the very best client experience possible.

I believe there are three key areas that you, as a business owner, must focus on, to deliver a consistently valuable experience to the client. These are as follows:

- Before the sale;

- During the sale, and;

- After the sale.

Let us discuss each stage in detail.

Before the sale

As we discussed earlier, with so many choices, as a potential client I can take my business virtually anywhere and, especially, when I'm deciding on that first, initial, purchase. You therefore need to create the ultimate 'client experience' from the very moment someone makes an initial enquiry with your business, and not when they receive the finished product or service.

Let's imagine the conversation going on inside your prospect's head. Your prospect will be feeling all kinds of emotions when considering doing business with you: they might feel wary, sceptical or threatened. Therefore you have a great opportunity to re-set your prospect's perception of you, your business and the results you can provide from the very moment they make that first initial contact.

So the key then is to offer a tremendous education up front. That is, rather than using a very 'sales orientated' message, you begin to educate your audience from the very start, as to how you appreciate and understand their concerns and frustrations. Offer some valuable insight from the very beginning that enables the prospect to have a much greater confidence in buying from you.

Keep this in mind: education builds rapport, cold direct selling breaks rapport. So before any transaction has taken place use every opportunity to demonstrate your expertise.

During the sale

Building on the above concept, it's important to see how you can offer a better client experience during the sale.

Try this strategy: plot every interaction you have with a client during the delivery of your product or service and then see how you're able to offer greater value at each stage.

Do not worry so much about the 'how' at this stage, that is, how you are going to offer this added value. For the time being concentrate on the 'what' i.e. what can you bring to the course of the transaction. For example during the course of delivering your product or service, where are the typical 'pain points' for your client?

Let your mind come up with all manner of opportunities and then see which are the most practical and cost-effective for your business.

After the sale

Finally, how can you add more value to your client's experience after the sale?

Look at how you approach your 'after sales service', or for that matter, look at how your industry or sector approaches this. Do you simply deliver the product or service, and then leave the client to it? Do you keep in regular contact after the sale and maybe offer additional help? For example, you may be in a position to offer a cross or up-sell to a complimentary product or service. Be mindful of what you feel the market would be most receptive to. This is not a strategy whereby you consistently harass the client for more business.

This small shift in how you approach 'customer service' will present you with so many opportunities.

Perception is reality

Rightly or wrongly, prospects make assumptions. It's one thing to state that you are an authority in your field; however it is even more important to demonstrate and articulate this. From your business cards, to your website, to how you dress, from the language you use, even down to the price you charge: your marketing, your 'posture' will always be taken at face value. Perception is reality. Or to be more exact, perception – in the eyes of your prospect – is reality.

So in the final part of this chapter, I want to give you some practical suggestions as to what you can actually put 'out there' to demonstrate trust, credibility and 'expert status.'

Firstly I would urge every business owner, no matter what industry they are in, to get into the habit of writing. Get into the routine of authoring specific reports or guides that articulate and communicate your particular take on an issue or challenge that your prospect often faces. By educating your audience, you automatically position yourself as a credible authority in your field. And just as important, you become associated with the education you provide.

Do remember to write about topics that your prospect is actually interested in. Let's take a very simple example. Say you're an accountant looking to position yourself as 'a trusted adviser'. You would want to avoid dry subjects such as corporation tax. Instead, you might want to discuss, say, the ten ways that your clients could decrease their tax bill. Same information, only articulated in such a way that it means something to your audience.

If you're stuck for ideas look at your industry press, look at industry online forums or bulletin boards. What themes keep coming up on a regular basis? What are currently the hot topics for debate?

If you're still struggling for ideas, then try this. Take a subject matter that you know will resonate with your audience, then give this topic a number i.e. "The 5 Ways To Overcome..." or "The 5 Challenges Faced By Every XXX" or "The 5 Secrets That Every XXX Should Know". You not only have a compelling title, you also have (in this example) five sub topics to develop and discuss. Many years ago I used to run a career consultancy, so I put together a short report called "The 5 Secrets Almost Every Recruitment Agency Doesn't Want You To Know!". This was a great positioning tool, as well as a good way of generating leads.

Writing shouldn't be seen as something that you almost have to force yourself to do, but seen as something that is an integral part of your overall positioning plan.

Similarly, look for ways in which you can demonstrate your expertise through different mediums. Different formats might appeal more to different audiences. Could you record a short audio on a topic that would appeal to your industry? Or, maybe you could record yourself being interviewed. Then maybe use this interview as a method for generating leads.

Maybe you could video yourself giving a presentation, or record yourself delivering some training. Again, none of this has to be costly. With advances in technology you don't have to spend a small fortune doing this, and nor do you want to.

Imagine the scenario now: I visit your website and I can download a short guide, or series of guides. Or there is an interview you have recorded that discusses ways of overcoming some of the key challenges your prospect faces. Again, as a visitor I might not necessarily read, download or listen to everything; however it's the perception that you demonstrate. Compare this to a 'traditional' website in your field, which is simply full of copy focused on you and your business. Of these two examples, who do you think I'm more likely to want to do business with?

It's the perception that matters most. It's one thing to state that you are an expert or an authority in your field, however it is even more important to demonstrate this. Get into the habit of generating educational material and offering it to your audience.

I would like to leave you with one, final, key principle that will govern your success: making the decision to 'go'. In other words, making the decision to consistently practice and apply the strategies that will help differentiate your company within your industry, sector or niche.

Deciding you want to be regarded as a leader in your field, the preferred choice, and then act accordingly. So embrace these strategies and tactics and then implement them!

Andrew Ludlam BA (Hons)
Expertise focus: Marketing

Andrew Ludlam is the owner of Maverick Marketing Consultancy, and is recognised as an expert on advanced marketing strategy and tactics. As a consultant, trainer, copywriter and author, he has advised many hundreds of business owners one-to-one, and many more have attended his private training programmes.

Andrew also publishes a fortnightly newsletter which has some 2,000 subscribers.

Special offer for *Breaking the Barriers to Business Growth* readers:
In this chapter "The Principle of Pre-Eminence", I introduced you to three strategies to help position yourself as the 'preferred choice' in your industry. If you would like to receive an additional seven strategies, then please email me directly at andrew@maverickmarketingconsultancy.co.uk to claim your free report, "10 Ways to Establish Yourself as an Expert and Gain Credibility in Any Industry".

Chapter 12

Networking

Cathy Dunbabin

Networking
Cathy Dunbabin

Introduction

Successful networking is not measured by the volume of business cards collected, the quantity of conversations had nor the number of meetings attended. It is measured by the quality of introductions, opportunities and business received.

Have you ever wasted hours drinking coffee, shaking hands, smiling politely whilst engaging in pointless conversation or sat through meetings where you felt the tax return was looking more appealing? If the answer is 'yes' then it's definitely time to rethink your approach to networking.

In 2009/10 over 80% of my business came from networking alone. Networking has the power to transform your business too.

Networking is a key marketing activity which will generate new clients and customers. Any size of business can benefit, from new start-ups to established companies. It works no matter what your product or service. Networking is incredibly powerful in enabling individuals access to markets through like-minded professionals who are willing, and more importantly able, to make introductions on their behalf. Now here comes the catch…

No one who has achieved anything of value did it without putting in time and effort. They've been willing to learn from experts and been prepared to research, plan and practice. If you want to get results, real tangible results, from your networking then you too need to be prepared to do the same.

In this chapter my goal is to highlight the potential benefits networking can offer your business. We will uncover the steps that enable successful networkers to receive an inordinate amount of business. The easiest way for me to do this is to share my networking strategy with you!

Taking the first step…

Once you have made the decision to include networking as part of your strategic marketing activity you need to do a bit of research. It's imperative to find the most appropriate networking group for you and your business – one size does not fit all!

Make sure you know what you wish to achieve from your networking. Decide your primary objective:

- To gain confidence and for self-development
- Meet other business owners and share their support and advice
- Meet service or product suppliers
- Improve the way you run your business
- Gain regular valuable business
- Grow your business and increase the turnover

When you have identified your personal objectives, search for local networking groups and arrange to visit them. Before making a final decision to join one ask yourself the following questions:

- Can I make the meeting times and attend regularly?
- Was the format and content congruent with my objectives?
- Are the businesses involved ones that I could potentially refer to?
- Do the current members have contacts with my ideal clients and introducers?
- What are the tangible benefits: referrals, support, personal development?
- Can I uphold all required commitments of membership?
- Was there a positive feel to the event, did I enjoy it and would I look forward to going again?

Once you have decided to join a group you must commit to engage fully. In order to get the most from it you must be prepared not only to put the time aside to attend the meetings but to do a bit of leg work too! An 'I'll give it a go' attitude will be detrimental to your success.

Successful networkers have many attributes: taking action and a positive attitude are just two of them.

Setting realistic goals...

Setting goals and measuring them seems fairly obvious. If you don't do this how do you know whether you are achieving your objectives?

Over the years I have met so many people who do not enjoy or benefit from their networking experience. Almost without exception they didn't set goals. Sadly they then become scarred and make generalised statements about networking being a "waste of time". When you set networking goals think about your quality products and services and set goals to promote these. A printer can close many deals for business cards or close one deal for producing a catalogue and achieve the same levels of financial reward. Apart from making more effort to deliver hundreds of business cards rather than the catalogues he can also become known for lower end work. Before he knows it that is what the group sees him as and his opportunities for larger contracts diminish. Seek out opportunities that will make a difference and transform your business. Networking is about quality, not quantity.

Successful networkers have many attributes: they always set networking goals and measure results.

Making the commitment...

As I mentioned at the beginning of this chapter, networking, like most things in life, is founded on getting out what you put in. There is no magic! It is not a quick fix for business growth! I get incredibly frustrated when I speak to members who settle for simply covering their costs. The real cost of networking is not the membership fees but the time required to implement it properly.

In the early days you will need to be prepared to spend a lot of time getting to know fellow members. This is essential in order to develop and nurture strong relationships.

The level of rewards you receive will be commensurate with the level of commitment you give. Therefore the higher the potential rewards a group offers the higher the level of involvement on your part.

Building those relationships...

Relationships are at the core of all successful networking. Many an accountant has questioned the purchase of a set of golf clubs under business expenses to be told, "The golf course is where I do my best business". The key to longevity and continuous referrals does not lie in selling to fellow members but in building valuable relationships that result in the abundant sharing of contacts.

Like all relationships, building them takes time and energy; getting on and liking each other is a good place to start. If a person is going to put their reputation on the line by making a recommendation they want to know their confidence and trust has been well placed. They will want to feel confident that a professional first class service will be provided. The more time you spend getting to know each other the more quickly this level of trust will be achieved.

When you first meet new contacts in a networking environment there will be an element of small talk. This stage is about building rapport and lays the first building blocks of a business relationship. It is about getting on, NOT pedalling your wares. Open-ended questions (who, what, how, when, where and why) can be particularly useful.

Don't be too keen to rush things! As you move forward, trust and credibility will develop and a desire and willingness to help will follow. When you have reached this level you will want to proactively seek and give introductions to each other's contacts. LinkedIn and databases are a great place to start. Put some time aside now, take a good look at your own contacts – who are you currently building business relationships with that would value an introduction to them? Have one to ones with fellow members, take your laptop and explore each other's contacts for opportunities.

Successful networkers have many attributes: they are intuitive, great listeners and readily build rapport.

Refining your presentation skills...

In my experience this is one area where many people struggle. It is so easy to try to include reams of information; after all you probably have a lot you want to say. However, too much information dilutes and confuses your message. Whether a 1, 5 or 10 minute slot, this is an opportunity to whet the appetite of your audience. The acid test of your presentation is whether it leads to a positive, productive action.

These are some key points to follow:-

Start positively

Jump to your feet and be passionate in your delivery. Avoid openers like "I never know what to say at this point" and "Now it's my turn to send you to sleep".

Only include necessary information

Your audience wants to know WIIFM (What's In It For Me). They are not interested, at this stage, about the location of your office or how many employees you have or even how long you have been trading. You will get plenty of time to tell people more of your history when you meet them on a one to one basis.

Include stories and pain

In this short presentation you are looking to ignite interest. Stories of success or pain prevention are extremely valuable as people can relate to them. It is important to talk about the benefits your clients receive as opposed to how you operate. Resonating with the listener will result in an opportunity for further discussions.

Call to action

If you want people to do something about what they have heard – enlighten them on what it is! This might sound obvious but the majority of networkers who don't get an outcome, usually forgot to ask for one. If you'd like an introduction to a specific company name the person you'd like to meet. If you have an email newsletter, invite people to subscribe to it but don't spam everyone who was there, it will only damage your reputation!

Memorable content and finishes

When an audience hears a number of presentations it becomes difficult to remember the detail. Humour and a memorable finish will embed the message.

LESS is MORE

Three Ps

Preparation should be as much about **P**lanning and research as much as **P**ractice. If you can, have a look at who will be present and tailor your message accordingly. Practice will help with the delivery and timing of your presentation; use a mirror to practice or if you are feeling brave enough ask a member of your family or a friend to listen to you. Remember you will always make a first impression… make it a great one!

Successful networkers have many attributes: the ability to deliver a compelling, memorable message others can relate to.

Don't forget to follow up and say thank you…

Whatever you have committed to do – do it! Whether it is to make an introduction, call to arrange a coffee or simply send some useful information to someone – make sure you do it. Stay in touch with your contacts. Be organized and use a CRM system or spreadsheet which will allow you to systemise keeping in touch and make it less likely you will forget.

When someone goes out of their way for you whether it be that they made an introduction or sent you some interesting information, do remember to thank them and tell them how much you appreciate it. Try to do something back for them, ask them what would be useful. Relationships are built on trust and trust is strengthened by selfless acts of goodwill. There is no bigger disappointment than putting yourself out for someone and they do not have the good manners to update or thank you.

Successful networkers have many attributes: a proactive, positive approach to creating opportunities.

Summary

Some of you may be thinking 'so what's new, we've heard all that before'… and you'd be right. Networking is not difficult! It occasionally suffers bad press, usually from those who aren't prepared to embrace a networking strategy. Are you going to let someone else's shortcomings hold you back? Take your networking seriously because it can dramatically transform your business.

Successful networkers have many attributes: they are generous, abundant and gain trust quickly.

Cathy Dunbabin
Expertise Focus: Business Networking

Cathy Dunbabin is a well-known face within the networking arena across Oxfordshire. She is passionate about using networking to transform businesses. Her own networking adventure began when, as a Mum returning to work, she ventured across the threshold and into her first networking meeting at 6.30 on a cold wet March morning back in 2002. With a few deep breaths and a stern talk to herself she quelled her nerves, dismissed the overwhelming urge to make a run for it and found herself in a room full of business owners, mainly men, drinking coffee and chatting.

Over the past 10 years Cathy has participated in an array of different styles of networking. She became an Assistant Director for a large networking organisation. Last year she was awarded 'Outstanding performance as an AD' at their European Conference. She has listened to, worked with and learned from some of the country's most prolific networkers. Nowadays it is Cathy giving the interviews and being asked to speak by other networking groups. She adds a fun and sometimes risqué slant on key networking skills.

In January 2011, Cathy launched Opendoorz, a networking opportunity for high calibre businesses focusing on building strong relationships that translate into genuine opportunities. For Cathy it's all about quality not quantity! Cathy has developed her networking skills by watching, listening and learning from others. Sign up to our blog www.opendoorz.wordpress.com for lots of Networking Knowhow.

Special offer to *Breaking the Barriers to Business Growth* readers:

One of my biggest frustrations is when I hear that networking is not working. Drop me a line and say hi to cathy@opendoorz.biz and I will be delighted to send you a copy of 'Networking – Awful to Awesome' a guide to getting results.

Chapter 13

Make sales without selling: practical sales techniques

David Winch

Make sales without selling: practical sales techniques

David Winch

For many professional service providers, selling is a 'necessary evil' you have to do to stay in business but something you dread.

'Handling objections' and 'closing the sale' may bring you out in a cold sweat, but once you discover you can make a sale without 'selling' and get paid what you're worth, this will stop and you will have a new skill to break your barriers to business growth.

The 'Sales Without Selling' method will show you how to create and confidently deliver a win-win pricing and selling strategy and bank most of your fee before you ever start work.

The 30 practical techniques in this article will introduce you to the concept of Selling without Selling and will guide you to where you can get more information.

How to think about your fees

Base your fee on the value the client gets out of what you do.

If your client is aware of the value they will get from achieving their objectives, they will view your fee as an investment to secure that return. If the 'return on investment' is big enough, it will present a compelling reason for using your services.

Charge different fees for different value.

If you did some work for a £1 million company that added £250,000 to their bottom line, and then helped a £10 million company save £25,000, isn't it reasonable that the smaller company should pay approximately 10 times more than the larger company?

There's nothing illegal or underhand in this; it's both moral and ethical – even if the work is similar. The client has agreed to make what they (correctly) believe to be a very reasonable investment to achieve a valuable return.

Ignore the past – it doesn't matter. Previous dealings with other service providers, payment by the day, are irrelevant.

They are dealing with you today and this is the way you work. Charging according to value is better for the client than paying for chunks of your time. It puts the client in total control of their costs.

Your value to your client has nothing to do with the time you put in. Your client has confirmed the value they will receive when you deliver as agreed. Do not feel guilty about receiving a high fee when the client sees it as a huge return for a reasonable investment. Your value is in your talent, not in your time.

Don't get greedy on the first sale – concentrate on lifetime revenue and **profit**.

Your goal is to develop a relationship and get follow on work from each of your clients.

Think strategically and think how you can help your client in the future.

Don't concede without trading.

Virtually every client concern will either be about value or price. Be aware that "It's too expensive" is a value concern, not a price concern.

Remember that "A different package can command a different price; a different price mandates a different package." Unilateral conceding is something you must not do.

Maintain your price by adding something you know the client will find of value. If your price is genuinely unaffordable for the client, discuss what can be left out to justify that lower price.

Free is better than low price.

Selling at, or even quoting, a low fee undermines value. You will become known as a 'low price provider'. Stick to your guns and quote a fee that provides a good return on investment.

If you feel you really want the work, or feel the client deserves your help more than most, but the price is not affordable, offer to do it for no fee at all, but I suggest you restrict these activities to registered charities and not-for-profit organisations.

Still present an invoice for the free stuff.

Always send an invoice for pro bono work because it will show the client what your fee would have been had you not waived it. This establishes your position for anyone within the client organisation or elsewhere who may get to hear of the work you've done for no charge.

'Supply and Demand' is irrelevant in your market.

Some people may insist the law of supply and demand works everywhere; this is both erroneous and counter-productive. Supply and demand applies to commodity markets; the last thing you want to be is a commodity. To increase your income you need to work smarter not harder. This means you raise your fees whilst working the same or fewer hours.

Be aware of 'Market Rates'.

You need to know market rates to know where you will position your services: as a Rolls Royce, a Mini, a 4x4 or a sports car. Knowing where you are and where you aren't competing is vital. Consider being the highest priced provider in that sector.

How to uncover value

Establish value in partnership with the prospective client.

Don't talk about how you might 'add value' – only your client can tell you, once they have understood the full value they will derive from achieving their objectives and the difference your help will make.

One of the skills you must acquire is the ability to help your client identify this value.

Engage the prospect in the 'diagnosis'.

The questions you ask the client in the process of understanding the value they will derive are really aimed at information gathering and helping them identify where they need your help.

When you work together on the diagnosis and ask the client's opinion there is greater 'buy in' from the client. We rarely disagree with our own opinions!

Never deal with the purchasing department! And only allow accounts payable to pay your account!

You must insist that you and the client wanting to buy your services absolutely agree on terms, responsibilities, scope, timescales, fees and all the rest.

Handing over to another department is only fine if all they are doing is implementing the paperwork and processing your payment.

Get the prospect to tell you their objectives as early as possible.

By getting to the "Where do we want to get to?" question at the start of the conversation, you ensure the client is focused on the results and not on the costs.

Kicking off with "Can we start with what you want to achieve as a result of this?" is a simple and valuable introduction, followed by "Why is that important?"

Broaden objectives to increase value.

Check the rigidity of any boundaries the client is placing on their objectives.

If the aim is to grow sales in the Home Counties by 10%, ask why they wouldn't want to grow across the whole country, and maybe by 15%.

Don't get stereotyped.

A niche is good for lead generation, but in a sales conversation it's important not to get stereotyped. Indicate other things you can do by referring to doing them for other clients. Being stereotyped is fee-limiting.

Always establish your personal value.

Scarcity, limited timescale and limited choice all increase value. Ask yourself "Why me?" "Why now?" and "Why this way?"

Knowing the answers to these three questions allows you to set your fee accordingly.

Look constantly for other opportunities.

The time to 'market' yourself is always now.

Value can be intangible as well as tangible; subjective as well as objective

You may have to push a little to get the client to fully articulate value. You, however, may need to 'monetise' the value. Once told the result would be "priceless" or "invaluable", move on.

Focus on improvement, not problem solving.

Many others may be able to solve the client's problems. Very few are able to lift the performance of a high flyer and make their performance truly world beating. This is where huge "Why me?" value lies.

Align yourself with innovation and performance improvement, not with problem solving, and the worth of your projects will rise accordingly.

How to prevent objections

Remove fees from all your printed and on-line materials.

Don't publish the fees for the major items you provide.

But if your way of getting business is to give some of your knowledge for free, then of course you should say so, and possibly add the price that you should be charging.

Always make clear whether expenses are extra or included.

It's for you to decide.

Don't quote your fee too early.

It is not unusual to be asked, "But how much is it going to cost me?" If you don't handle this correctly, you can totally blow your chances of succeeding with these techniques. Your only possible response is, "I don't know. It's far too early to say at this time. Please can we get back to talking about your.... and I'll tell you my fee when we're clearer what help is needed."

Don't accept 'troublesome' business.

If prospective clients are awkward, nasty or unethical before or during the sales conversation, gracefully walk away. Bad business is worse than no business.

Cull the bottom 15% of your clients regularly.

Refer these clients to someone else who will appreciate and handle them even better than you. You'll be free to secure more of the clients you relish.

Don't allow 'scope creep': new work is a new project and requires a new proposal.

Make sure you and your client have agreed on the specifics of the project. Any extra work outside the objectives of the original agreement is a new project so requires a new proposal and it will naturally be subject to a new fee.

This new project needs to be prioritised relative to the existing project.

You don't have to accept referral business on the same terms as the referrer.

Just because company 'A' pays consultant 'B' by the hour or after work is complete, this has no bearing on how they should pay you if consultant 'B' refers them to you.

Start with the payment terms most beneficial to you.

Once value is established, be the first to mention payment terms, and start with payment in full before work commences. If the client doesn't like this, offer 50% before you start and 50% 30 days later.

If you start with no down payment, the client has no huge reason to commit to the project.

Never accept terms based on sharing the results of your work.

Payment by results completely reverses the risk structure of time-based fees, and is just as bad. Conditions can change: buyers can be moved internally, leave or die. Projects can be 'not quite finished'. If you allow yourself to get caught like this, you deserve what you get, or don't get.

Ensure the client is aware that they should pay other suppliers directly.

Don't get sucked into sub-contracting arrangements – your client should pay suppliers directly.

Unless you already have clients begging to buy from you, you owe it to yourself to get better acquainted with 'Selling Without Selling'. I hope you enjoy adapting and testing many of these ideas, and that they bring you great success.

David Winch
Expertise Focus: Practical Selling, Marketing and Pricing

Many professional service providers such as business consultants, lawyers, accountants, independent software developers and any others who feel the only way to charge is for the time they spend working on their clients' projects, have two major problems. To a greater or lesser degree they don't like selling, and they also think they're not getting paid what they're worth.

I work with these professionals on setting prices so that their customers are delighted, and on making handsome profits. I help them understand how to sell in ways that get customers asking to buy and paying more, more quickly. Together we develop and implement practical marketing strategies to attract and retain the 'top-notch' customers in their markets. And having helped them with all this, I work with them until they have the confidence to do all these things themselves, every time. I call it "Selling Without Selling."

I have successfully used this process myself ever since I was taught the basics in early 2008. From the very start, I more than doubled my fees - and much more on several occasions. I also greatly increased my closing rate and started getting paid before work ever started. The reaction of my customers moved rapidly to "That's a bargain. How soon can you start?" Ever since then I have researched the subject extensively, becoming well known by the global experts in the field so that they now describe me as a UK expert.

Special offer to _Breaking the Barriers to Business Growth_ readers:
If you have liked my ideas on Selling Without Selling, you most probably would like to take it further. Selling Without Selling is wide-ranging but it is not difficult to achieve. The first requirement is a mind that is open to looking at traditional ways of doing things in a new light, and to trying out new ways.

To get you started I am offering you a copy of my "Pricing By Value" DVD. This DVD condenses a half-day workshop, normally priced at £250, into just 75 minutes of solid advice and practical help, for just £99.00 +VAT. Watch the workshop as many times as you like and get these practical ideas working in your business straight away. Order your copy now at www.davidwinch. co.uk/dvd_bbbg.htm